M I D I

Orchestrator Plus™

MIDI Sequencer and
Multitrack Recorder/Editor

You will need the Product ID number from the Registration Card when you install the software. You also will need this number if you phone for technical support. Please copy this number to the line below so you will have it for future reference!

Product ID Number: C M S 1 Ø Ø - Ø 1 5 6 7 4 - 1 5 7

MIDI Orchestrator Plus ™

To Contact Voyetra Technologies Inc.

By mail	Voyetra Technologies Inc.
	5 Odell Plaza
	Yonkers, NY 10701-1406 USA
Fax	914-966-1102
Bulletin Board	914-966-1216 N, 8, 1
CompuServe®	76702.2037
Sales and Information	800-233-9377
Sales	sales@voyetra.com
Information	info@voyetra.com
Technical Support	914-966-0600
Technical Support	support@voyetra.com
Website	http://www.voyetra.com
To Register Software	register@voyetra.com

To Register Your Software

You can register your software by mail, fax, phone, BBS or WWW.

May 1997• Part Number: 04530-M02• ISBN 1-888743-06-9

Using This Manual

This manual is designed to get you started using MIDI Orchestrator Plus as quickly as possible. The following strategy for using this manual — and the program — is suggested.

If MIDI is new to you, turn to the Appendix for an overview of the technology. This section will acquaint you with the concepts and terms you should know to work with the program.

The early chapters in this manual help you set up your computer and MIDI keyboard. A series of tutorials take you step-by-step through the basic techniques of using the software. The later chapters provide screen-by-screen, feature-by-feature reference information.

If you encounter any problems during installation or while using the software, run MediaCheck,™ Voyetra's diagnostic utility. It's included with MIDI Orchestrator Plus and installs automatically.

The Appendices at the back of the book contain useful information on MIDI and hardware and diagnostics. A list of Keyboard Shortcut Keys, the General MIDI Patch Set, General MIDI Drum Note Map and General MIDI Controller Types also can be found here.

To find information about a specific control, menu item or dialog box, refer to the Table of Contents at the front of the book or the comprehensive Index at the back.

Acknowledgments

This manual would not have become a reality without the many talented people who contributed to its creation.

Editorial
Ronni Geist, *Documentation Manager*
Robert Goodman
Uku Meri
Scott Walters

Graphics
Carlos Crespo
Keith Nitsch
Scott Walters

Production
Clifford A. Parms, *Production Director*
Andrew Toomey, *Project Coordinator*

Table of Contents

Chapter 8: Piano Roll Window

Appendix E: Troubleshooting   219

Appendix F: Technical Support   231

Index   232

Chapter 1

Getting Started...

Welcome!

Thank you for purchasing MIDI Orchestrator Plus.™ This program is one in a series of Voyetra Technologies' CD-ROM titles designed to bring professional-quality music recording and editing to multimedia computer users.

Voyetra Technologies has been in the business of music hardware and software for more than 20 years. We are the world's leading provider of interactive sound, audio and music multimedia software. Our software is included with many of the sound cards and PCs sold today, so there is a good chance you already own some of our other products.

Whether you are a new acquaintance or a Voyetra veteran, you will benefit from our long-standing upgrade policy and our excellent technical support.

As a registered user, you are entitled to special discounts on our other products — but we can't offer you these benefits if we don't know who you are! So before you install MIDI Orchestrator Plus, take a minute to register your software...and welcome to the Voyetra family!

On the World Wide Web

When you're "surfing the net," be sure to visit Voyetra's Website for the latest information on products and upgrades — www.voyetra.com

Benefits of Registering Your Software

There are many benefits to registering your software. In addition to our limited warranty, you'll also receive:

- **Update Notifications** — we'll keep you informed of software updates and new Voyetra products.
- **VoyeTracks™ Newsletter** — we'll let you know about developments at Voyetra Technologies, with information on how others are using our software and tips to help you get the most from our products.
- **Upgrade Plan** — we'll offer you discounts on Voyetra's full-featured PC sound products.
- **Technical Support** — we'll be happy to help you get your software installed before you register; however, you must be a registered user to receive full technical support.

You can register your software by mail, fax, phone, BBS, Internet or World Wide Web — whichever is easiest for you. See the front of this manual for these addresses.

What's Included

Here's what's included with MIDI Orchestrator Plus.

Software

- **MIDI Orchestrator Plus™**
  Use this full-featured MIDI sequencer to compose songs. Record MIDI tracks one instrument at a time to build songs. Edit your songs using standard Windows® drag-and-drop techniques. Then print sheet music on any Windows-compatible printer.

- **MediaCheck™**
  Test and troubleshoot the multimedia features of your computer. A series of displays takes you step-by-step through the testing process. If your system's multimedia devices are not working properly, MediaCheck provides troubleshooting tips.

Online Video Tutorials

We've included three video tutorials to help you become familiar with MIDI Orchestrator Plus.

- **MIDI Orchestrator Plus Tour**
  Takes you on a guided tour of the program's features.

- **Recording in MIDI Orchestrator Plus**
  Teaches you the basics of desktop MIDI recording.

- **Editing in MIDI Orchestrator Plus**
  Steps you through the techniques for editing your musical compositions.

Sample Files

To help you get started creating music quickly, we've included dozens of sample files which can be accessed from the CD-ROM.

- **Drum Tracks** (located in the demos\drumtrax directory)
  A variety of styles including pop, rock, jazz, funk and others.

- **MIDI Files** (located in the demos\midfiles directory)
  A selection of classical, action, rock, pop, religious and other styles.

And, to help you practice the basic techniques, we've included:

- **SAMPLE.ORC** (located in the Voyetra directory)
  A sample file to use with the tutorials in this manual.

Creating Music

You'll be amazed at the professional-sounding music you can create with MIDI Orchestrator Plus.

Load a sample MIDI file off the CD-ROM (demos\midfiles) and let your creative juices flow! Add a melody; lengthen or shorten sections. Change instruments; modify notes with transforms. Alter the song any way you wish. If you don't like the changes you've made, click Undo. Ready for something different? Change a classical piece into a heavy metal rocker!

There's no need to hammer out drum parts. With the sample drum files on the CD-ROM (demos\drumtrax), you have a professional drummer just a mouse-click away! Find a beat you like and bring the drum track into MIDI Orchestrator Plus. Now add additional parts. When you're done, print sheet music on any Windows-compatible printer!

Use MIDI Orchestrator Plus as a multitrack recorder to record as you play on your MIDI keyboard. Fool around! Be creative! Don't worry if you make a mistake — with MIDI Orchestrator Plus, it's easy to edit notes individually with your mouse.

Minimum Hardware Requirements

These are the *minimum* hardware requirements:

- IBM PC or compatible running Windows 3.1 or 95
- 486DX2/66 or higher processor
- 8 megabytes of RAM (Random Access Memory)
- SVGA monitor and adapter capable of displaying 640x480, at least 256 colors
- Hard disk drive with at least 5 Megabytes of free storage space
- Double-speed (or faster) CD-ROM drive
- Windows-compatible sound card
- MIDI-compatible musical keyboard
- Headphones or speakers connected to your sound card

Using the Software

All of your multimedia hardware and software must be working correctly **before** you install the software. If your system isn't working properly, neither will MIDI Orchestrator Plus!

You should have Microsoft Windows (3.1 or 95) installed and working on your computer.

You should have an external MIDI keyboard attached. (For information on connecting your MIDI keyboard, refer to "Setting Up Your MIDI Keyboard" in the following chapter.)

You should have headphones and/or speakers connected to the jack labeled "output" or "speakers" on the back of your sound card. If you are using speakers, they need to have their own amplification since the output from the sound card may be too low to power them. Speakers with built-in amps are powered either by battery or AC.

Working with Windows

MIDI Orchestrator Plus works with Microsoft Windows. To use MIDI Orchestrator Plus, you should know how to:

- Use the mouse to move the cursor, select items, click, double-click drag-and-drop.
- Work buttons, drop-down lists and other controls that appear on Windows screens.
- Find, open, name, save and close files.

If any of these techniques are unfamiliar to you, refer to your Windows manual or work through the tutorial included with Windows before proceeding.

Chapter 2

Up and Running

MIDI Orchestrator Plus has an automatic installation process.

To Install the Software:

1. Make certain you have the Product ID number. This number can be found on the Registration Card. (Be certain to copy the Product ID number to the front of this manual so you will have it available should you need to phone for Technical Support.)

2. Place the CD in your computer's CD-ROM drive.
    *   For Windows 3.1, choose Run from the Program Manager's File menu.
    *   For Windows 95, choose Run from the Taskbar's Start menu. (When you insert the MIDI Orchestrator Plus disc for the first time in Windows 95, you are automatically prompted to run it.)

3. In the Run dialog box, type the letter of the drive followed by \setup. If your CD-ROM drive is d:, type **d:\setup**. Press Enter.

4. Follow the on-screen instructions.

 During installation, Indeo video drivers must be installed. If you view the Indeo README file during the install, it will appear as though you quit the installation before it was complete. However, this is not the case. MIDI Orchestrator Plus will fully install.

README File

During installation, a README file containing important information, will be installed. We recommend you read this information before you proceed.

To View the README File:

1. Double-click on the README icon.
2. In Windows 3.1, Windows Write will open and display the file. In Windows 95, WordPad will open and display the file.
3. To print the README file, choose Print from the File menu of either Windows Write or WordPad.

Running the Software

Each application — MediaCheck, MIDI Orchestrator Plus, the Voyetra Product Catalog — has its own icon in the Voyetra program group.

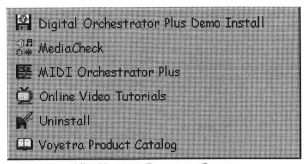

The Voyetra Program Group

MIDI Orchestrator Plus gets installed to your hard drive; however, to run MediaCheck, the Online Video Tutorials, or the Voyetra catalog, the disc must be in your CD-ROM drive.

Uninstalling MIDI Orchestrator Plus

There is no need to uninstall MIDI Orchestrator Plus before installing a new version of the software! Should you decide to remove MIDI Orchestrator Plus from your hard drive, the included Uninstall utility allows you to do so easily. But be careful! Uninstall removes everything — even files you have created — from the \MOP directory.

 Uninstall will remove everything in your MOP (MIDI Orchestrator Plus) directory — even files you have created which were not part of the original program.

Be certain to carefully read the on-screen instructions before running Uninstall!

Online Video Tutorials

MIDI Orchestrator Plus comes with a three online tutorials which help you learn about the software. You can watch these right on your computer monitor. Now is a good time to watch the first video.

To View the First Video:

1. Put the MIDI Orchestrator Plus disc in the CD-ROM drive.
2. Click the Online Video Tutorial icon in the Voyetra program group.
3. Click ❶ MIDI Orchestrator Plus Tour.
4. Sit back, relax, and enjoy the video!

Setting Up Your MIDI Keyboard

To fully utilize the features of MIDI Orchestrator Plus, you'll need to have a MIDI keyboard properly connected to your PC. A MIDI adapter cable attaches the keyboard to your PC. This cable uses the joystick port on your sound card as a MIDI interface. One end of the cable has a multipin connector which attaches to the sound card. The other end of the cable has two connectors — MIDI In and MIDI Out — which are connected to the MIDI keyboard.

Making the Connections

The following illustration describes how to connect the MIDI cable.

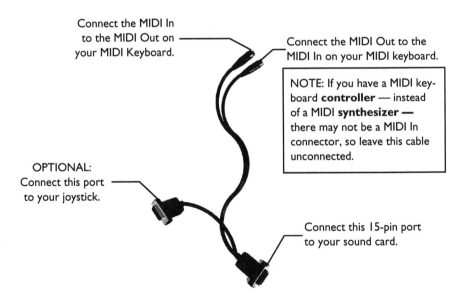

Connect the MIDI In to the MIDI Out on your MIDI Keyboard.

Connect the MIDI Out to the MIDI In on your MIDI keyboard.

NOTE: If you have a MIDI keyboard **controller** — instead of a MIDI **synthesizer** — there may not be a MIDI In connector, so leave this cable unconnected.

OPTIONAL: Connect this port to your joystick.

Connect this 15-pin port to your sound card.

 To view a video which demonstrates how to connect the MIDI adapter cable, see "MIDI Cable Installation Video" which follows.

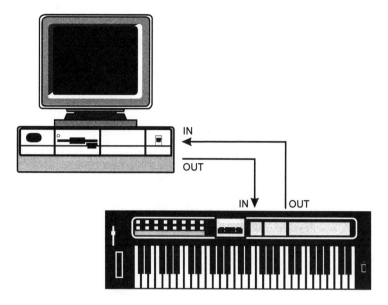

Typical MIDI setup with a musical keyboard.

MIDI Cable Installation Video

We've included a video which demonstrates how to connect a MIDI cable. This video is in MediaCheck.

To View the Video:

1. Put the MIDI Orchestrator Plus disc in the CD-ROM drive.
2. In the Voyetra program group, click the icon for MediaCheck.
3. In MediaCheck, click Setup Tips at the bottom left of the screen.
4. When asked if you want to view instructions on setting up your external keyboard, click Yes.
5. Sit back and watch the video!

Configuring MIDI Orchestrator Plus

Complete the steps below to configure MIDI Orchestrator Plus.

To Configure the Software:

1. Click the MIDI Orchestrator Plus icon to start the program.
2. Select MIDI Port Setup from the Options menu to display the MIDI Port Setup dialog box.

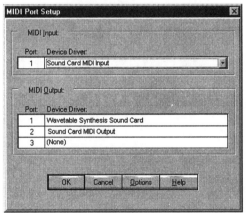

The Device Drivers displayed on your screen will be specific to your system and may differ from those appearing here.

3. Select Port 1 and choose the MIDI Input for your sound card and/or MIDI interface. If you have more than one physical MIDI input device, select the others accordingly for the additional input ports.
4. We recommend that instead of using Windows MIDI Mapper, you select whichever of the available output ports you intend to use as individual ports. This will make your routings easier to use and all channels will be available for each of the ports.

If you encounter any difficulties, run MediaCheck, Voyetra's multi-media diagnostic program.

Chapter 3

Overview

The Windows in MIDI Orchestrator Plus

The Main Window

MIDI Orchestrator Plus has a Main window in which a variety of sub-windows display MIDI data. These are all located in an area referred to as the Workspace.

These sub-windows let you view the MIDI data in different ways — each of which facilitates accomplishing a specific task. You can open and close the sub-windows and switch freely between them.

The top and bottom of the Main window also contain the most commonly used tools and displays. These include the Menu, Transport bar and Status bar. These controls are always available, no matter which window is currently active.

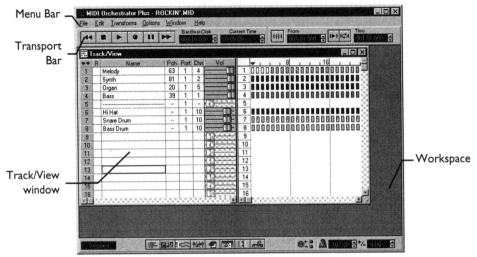

Menu Bar

Transport Bar

Track/View window

Workspace

Status Bar (along the bottom of the screen) with Quick View Buttons

The Main window showing the Menu and Transport Bars (along the top) and the Status Bar (at the bottom). These controls are always visible. Various editing windows can be opened in the Workspace at the center of the screen. In this example, the Track/View window occupies the Workspace.

Menu Bar

A standard Menu Bar contains all of MIDI Orchestrator Plus' control menus. Clicking a menu title drops down its menu list, from which you can choose from the available commands. Not all of the menu selections apply to all of the windows. When a menu selection is not applicable to the active window or the data currently selected, the menu command is unavailable (grayed out).

Transport Controls

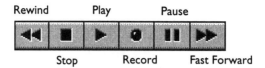

Rewind   Play   Pause

Stop   Record   Fast Forward

The Transport Controls are used for playing and recording music. The buttons resemble standard VCR or tape deck controls.

Other controls on this bar let you select a segment of a musical file for playback or recording.

 If you haven't already viewed the MIDI Orchestrator Plus Tour video tutorial, now would be a good time to do so!

- *Put the MIDI Orchestrator Plus CD in the CD-ROM drive.*
- *Click the Video Tutorial icon in the Voyetra program group.*
- *Then click* ❶ *MIDI Orchestrator Plus Tour.*

Status Bar and Quick View Buttons

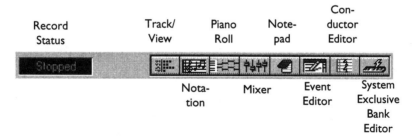

Record Status   Track/View   Piano Roll   Note-pad   Con-ductor Editor

Nota-tion   Mixer   Event Editor   System Exclusive Bank Editor

The Status Bar at the bottom of the screen displays the Record Status monitor and the Quick View buttons. Clicking on the Quick View buttons provides fast, easy access to the eight sub-windows in MIDI Orchestrator Plus.

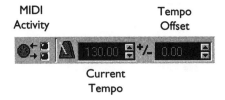

MIDI
Activity

Tempo
Offset

Current
Tempo

Other indicators on the Status Bar include MIDI Activity, Current Tempo and Tempo Offset.

Workspace

MIDI Orchestrator Plus' editing windows are opened in an area called the Workspace — the center portion of the screen. Each window provides a different view of the musical data.

Although you can have many editing windows open at once, only one can be the active window. Whenever you click on a window, it becomes the active window and its Title Bar is highlighted. When you have several windows open, you can tell which window is active by looking at its Title Bar. The commands and controls in the menus, Transport Bar and Status Bar affect the data in the currently active editing window.

How the Program Is Organized

MIDI Orchestrator Plus manipulates MIDI data in independent tracks, similar to those on a multitrack tape recorder. Once music is recorded onto a MIDI track, you can re-record, duplicate, copy, delete, change patches (instruments) or manipulate the data anywhere in the track. This allows you to compose songs one part at a time — in real time — or one note at a time by assigning one MIDI instrument per track.

The Windows

Here is an overview of the various windows:

Track/View window provides control of track parameters.

Notation window controls printing of your MIDI files in standard musical notation

Piano Roll window is best for editing individual notes.

Mixer window offers overall control of a song at the channel level.

Notepad window allows text to be included in a file.

Event Editor window gives precise control over the finest details of a single note or controller event.

Conductor Editor window controls the song's Tempo, Meter, and Key Signature.

System Exclusive Bank Editor window lets you send, receive and edit SysEx messages.

There is no right or wrong way to use the program — but, as you can see, certain windows are especially suited to particular tasks.

The tutorials in the following chapter are designed to show you which window is best for each procedure.

We encourage you to experiment and to develop your own working methods as you gain experience using the software.

Track/View Window

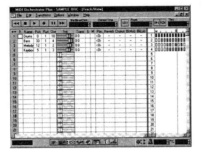

The Track/View window provides a "track sheet" for your MIDI song. Each track contains data for each instrument and assigns that instrument to a MIDI channel. The track sheet condenses a large amount of information into a small area, allowing you to organize, edit, re-arrange and name all instrument assignments.

The parameters you can set of adjust from this screen include: Volume, Pan, Key, Port, Solo, Mute, and Upper & Lower Bank Select.

Notation Window

The Notation window displays and prints sheet music in standard notation directly from MIDI song files. Notation includes many professional features and options such as quantization, rest suppression, angled beaming, multiple tracks and staves.

In this window, you can also format the title of the song, the author's name and copyright notice.

However, you **cannot** edit musical notation in this window. To change a printed score, you must use the Piano Roll and Event List Editor to change the underlying MIDI data.

Piano Roll Window

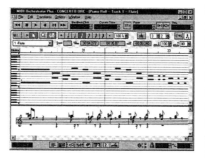

In this window, you access individual notes for any track and scroll backwards or forwards in the song. Audible "scrubbing" lets you to hear the notes as you move the cursor over them. Just click-and-drag in the Ruler bar while pressing the right-mouse button. Audition notes as you insert them or hear them by clicking with the arrow tool.

You can double-click on any note in this window to display its parameters. This permits editing at a very detailed level.

Clicking the right-mouse button in the editing area brings up a menu which lets you select tools and options quickly.

Mixer Window

The Mixer window resembles a studio mixer console. It provides a mixing console layout, with a module to adjust volume, pan, solo, mute and other parameters for each of the 16 channels on a single MIDI port. You also can select and adjust two MIDI controllers for all 16 channel modules.

The Mixer window gives you a quick and easy way to balance volumes and try out patch and controller settings. You can control each of the 16 channels for each of the Ports selected in the Options/MIDI Output Port.

Notepad

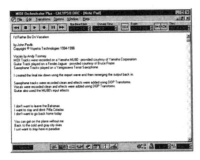

The Notepad is a handy place to store such text-based information as file's name, author and copyright information, production notes, tempo and other settings, song lyrics, and so on. Any text you type in this window is saved as part of the MIDI file.

Event Editor Window

The Event List, in the Event Editor window, lets you examine and edit raw MIDI data at its most basic level.

This window includes every MIDI command in the file: notes, controllers, embedded patch changes, pitch bends, aftertouch, and so on.

If you know the type of command you're seeking but don't want to search through every command in the file, you can filter the data so the window displays only the type(s) of MIDI data you wish to see.

Conductor Editor Window

The Conductor Editor functions very similarly to the Event Editor. However, with the Conductor Editor, you have control over the global controls instead of editing the very fine details of a song. In this window, you can change the key signature, meter and the tempo.

Editing these parameters lets your songs contain both *accelerandos* and *ritardandos*, and you can edit the time and key signatures to print out complex scores accurately.

SysEx Window

The SysEx window is used in conjunction with synthesizers that are capable of generating and transmitting a special class of MIDI messages called System Exclusive (SysEx) messages. Among other things, these messages contain information about patch settings, MIDI configuration parameters and special effects settings like reverb and delay.

MIDI Orchestrator Plus lets you load these messages from your synthesizer, save the data as files, and send the messages back to your synthesizer so they will be available to the synth the next time your song plays.

Multiple Instances

Using multiple instances (additional copies) of a window can make editing large files easier. With several different views on screen, you can quickly cut-and-paste data from one screen to another.

- You can open multiple instances of the Mixer, Piano Roll, Event Editor and Notation window.
- You can only open a single instance of the Track/View, Conductor Editor, Notepad and SysEx windows.

Video Guided Tour

MIDI Orchestrator Plus comes with three Online Video Tutorials to help you see how the software works.

If you haven't already done so, now would be a good time to view the MIDI Orchestrator Plus Tour.

To View the Video:

1. Put the MIDI Orchestrator Plus disc in the CD-ROM drive.
2. Click the Video Tutorial icon in the Voyetra program group.
3. Click ❶ MIDI Orchestrator Plus Tour.
4. Sit back, relax, and watch the video!

Chapter 4

Tutorials

Hands-On Tour

It's time for a hands-on overview of MIDI Orchestrator Plus.

Here's a Hands-On Tour of the Software:

1. Open the program from Windows. The first time you open
    MIDI Orchestrator Plus, you'll see the Track/View editing
    window maximized inside the Workspace. This is the default
    setting.

2. Change the Track/View window to a sizable window by
    clicking on the Maximize (Restore to Window) button in the
    upper right corner of the Track/View window.

    You will notice that the Track/View window now occupies
    only a portion of the Workspace while the Main Program
    window, its menus, the Transport Bar and Status Bar controls
    remain the same. These controls are always available, regard-
    less of which editing window(s) you have open.

3. Click one or two of the Quick View buttons at the bottom of
    the screen. These buttons open different editing windows. The
    windows you have just opened will overlap the Track/View
    window.

4. Minimize some of the windows you have just opened by clicking the Minimize Window buttons in the upper right corners of the windows. You'll notice that the windows shrink to icon size and the icons arrange themselves at the bottom of the Workspace. This enables you to keep a number of windows accessible without clutter.

The Track/View and Piano Roll windows are open in the Workspace

Icons for other sub-windows are minimized

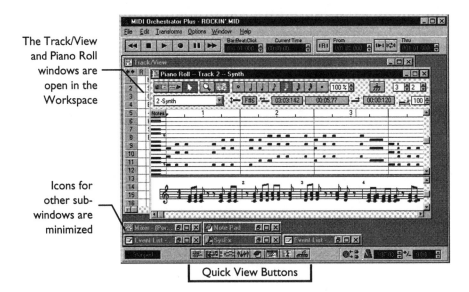

Quick View Buttons

The screen illustrated above shows Main program window with the Track/View and Piano Roll sub-windows open in the Workspace. Other editing windows have been minimized to icons at the bottom of the screen to keep the Workspace clear.

This is one way to view several sub-windows simultaneously. To configure your screen this way, select Cascade from the Windows menu. You can use standard Windows commands and mouse actions to open, re-size or minimize each window within the work area, and you can change the arrangement of windows as your work requires.

Opening Multiple Instances of a Window

The Quick View buttons in the Status bar at the bottom of the screen can be used to open the first instance of a window. Each of these buttons represents a different editing window.

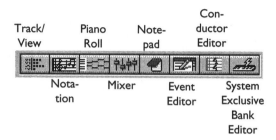

Track/   Piano   Note-   Con-
View   Roll   pad   ductor Editor

Nota-   Mixer   Event   System
tion   Editor   Exclusive Bank Editor

However, the Quick View buttons CANNOT be used to open multiple instances of editing windows. Instead, use the New command in the Window menu to open additional views of an editing window.

To Open Multiple Instances of a Window:

1. We'll begin by opening the Piano Roll Window. Click the Quick View button with the Piano Roll symbol on it — it's the third from the left at the bottom of the screen.

2. Click the Restore Window button in the upper right-hand corner of the Piano Roll window. The Piano Roll window becomes a smaller, sizable window in the Workspace.

3. Select New from the Window menu at the top of the screen and click Piano Roll. A second instance of the Piano Roll window opens and overlaps the first. You can open multiple instances of the Piano Roll, Event Editor and Mixer windows.

4. Click the Maximize button in the upper right-hand corner of the Track/View window so that the Track/View window again fills the Workspace.

- *Use either the Quick View buttons or the Window menu to open editing windows. The Quick View buttons are faster, but if you prefer to use the computer keyboard, you can use the menus.*

- *You cannot use the Quick View buttons to open multiple views of a window. Multiple instances can only be opened from the Window menu.*

- *Although you can open several instances of the Mixer, Piano Roll, and Event Editor windows, you can open only single instances of the Conductor Editor, Track/View, Notepad and SysEx windows.*

If You Need Help

MIDI Orchestrator Plus offers several forms of on-screen help.

Context-Sensitive Help

- If you have a MIDI Orchestrator Plus window open — for example, the Track/View window, Piano Roll window, Notepad, etc.— pressing F1 displays the Help Contents screen from which you can click on or search for specific help topics.

- If a dialog box is open or if you click on a menu item, pressing F1 displays context-sensitive help which directly corresponds to the feature or menu item you presently are accessing.

- To obtain help on using Help, press the F1 key twice.

One Line Help

- As you move the mouse around the screen, One Line Help presents a single-line definition of the screen areas and controls. This help information is displayed in the Title Bar at the top of the screen.

- One Line Help can be turned on and off by clicking on the words "One Line Help" in the Help menu. A check mark indicates that One Line Help is active.

Tool Tips

- Move the mouse so that the pointer rests atop a button or other on-screen control. After a second or two, a small, yellow window pops up to identify the name of the button or control on which the mouse pointer is resting. This is known as "Tool Tip" help.

- Tool Tips Help can be turned on and off by clicking on the words "Tool Tips" in the Help menu. A check mark indicates that Tool Tips is active.

Loading and Playing a File

Now that you are familiar with the various screens, let's get down to business. We'll begin by loading and playing a file. The file we'll be using is called SAMPLE.ORC.

To Load and Play a File:

1. Track/View should be maximized. (If it is not already the active window, switch to Track/View and maximize it by clicking the Maximize/Restore button at the upper right-hand corner of the screen.)

2. Open the File menu by using the mouse or by pressing the ALT and F keys (ALT+F) simultaneously on the computer keyboard.

3. Select Open from the File menu. The File Open dialog box displays. This is the standard Windows dialog box with one addition — the Audition button at the lower right. As its name suggests, this button lets you to listen to a file before opening it in the program.

4. If you're not already there, locate the Voyetra directory (C:\VOYETRA) and open the SAMPLE.ORC file by double-clicking it.

   When the file loads into the MIDI Orchestrator Plus screen, data appears in the rows numbered 1, 2, 3 and 4 at the left. This side of the screen is called the **Track Pane** and these numbers correspond to the tracks of the same names.

The right side of the screen is called the **Bar Pane**. The small rectangles (MIDI data boxes) represent bars of recorded MIDI music for the four tracks in this piece.

5. To play the file, click the Play button on the Transport Bar or press the Spacebar on your computer keyboard. While the music plays, a number of things happen:

    •   The numbers in the box labeled Bar:Beat:Click increase.

    •   The time in the Current Time indicator box increase.

    •   A red triangle ▼ called the Play Position pointer and its playback highlighting bar move from the left to the right, from bar to bar, to indicate which bar is being played.

    If you don't hear anything when you press Play, re-check the connections and the sound card mixer settings. If this doesn't resolve the problem, run Voyetra's MediaCheck™ diagnostic utility. See the Appendix for more information on MediaCheck.

6. To stop playback and reset the play position line at the beginning of the song, press the Spacebar or click the Stop button.

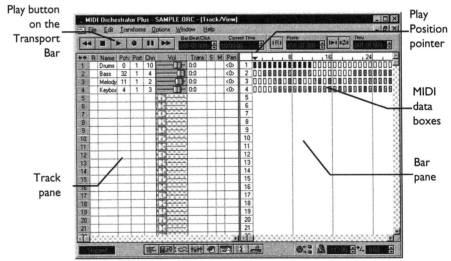

The Track/View window with SAMPLE.ORC. loaded.
The Track Pane is on the left. The Bar Pane is on the right.
The Play Position Pointer appears above the MIDI bars.

The Play Position Pointer

The Play Position pointer ▼ — a red triangle poised above the MIDI data boxes — shows at which measure the music will start when Play is clicked. By moving the Play Position Pointer, you can adjust the position at which the song will begin playing.

To Play SAMPLE.ORC from a Different Starting Point:

1. Open the SAMPLE.ORC file if it is not already open.
2. Click the right-mouse button at the number 8 just above the MIDI data boxes. This moves the Play Position pointer to the 8th bar of the song.
3. Tap the Spacebar. The song will start playing from the 8th bar.
4. Tap the Spacebar again to stop playback.

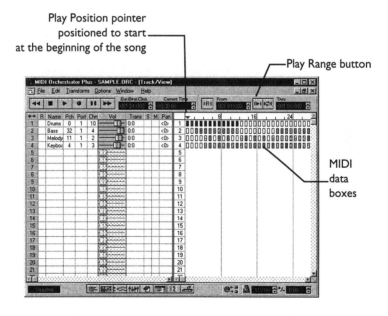

Play Position pointer positioned to start at the beginning of the song

Play Range button

MIDI data boxes

MIDI Data Boxes

Rectangles are used to represent the MIDI data for a track. The shading of the boxes represents the amount of data present.

- MIDI data boxes with no shading do not contain data.
- MIDI data boxes with heavy shading contain a lot of MIDI data.

Playing a Range and Looping

Suppose you want to play just a particular segment of music and have playback stop automatically at a particular point. Instead of using the Play Position pointer, you can use the mouse to select just the section of music you want to hear. The selected area is called a **range**.

- *A selected area is called a Range.*
- *To select a range, use traditional Windows' drag-and-select techniques.*
- *Replaying a range repeatedly is referred to as Looping.*

To Select a Range and Loop It:

1. Click the mouse cursor just to the left of the 5th MIDI data box of the top row in the Bar Pane.
2. Now hold down the left mouse button as you drag the mouse diagonally until you reach the end of bar 12 and you're at the bottom of the MIDI data boxes.
   - You'll notice that the bars have been selected and appear highlighted. This is the basic technique for selecting a range of a file. You'll be using this technique throughout the program.

3. Now that you've selected a range, locate the box labeled "From" in the Transport Bar. While holding down the Ctrl key on your computer keyboard, click the mouse button. (This is referred to as Ctrl-click.) You'll notice that the numbers in the From box change to 5:01:000. This shows that play starts at the beginning of the 5th bar.

4. Ctrl-click the Thru box as you did the From box. The numbers in the Thru box will change to 12:04:479, showing that the entire 12th bar is played last.

5. Now you can click the Play Range button just to the right of the From box. The Play Position pointer moves to bar 5 and only the selected portion of your file — eight measures — plays.

6. Press the Loop button (just to the left of the Thru box) to loop (repeatedly play) the range.

7. When you have heard enough, press the Spacebar to stop playing.

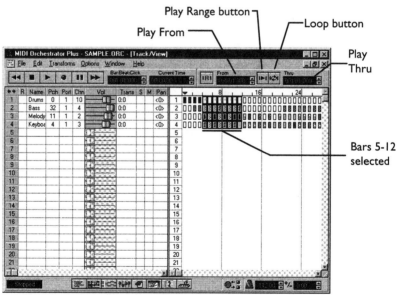

SAMPLE.ORC with the range of bars 5 through 12 selected for all tracks. The From and Thru boxes will show the Range if you Ctrl-click them.

Mute and Solo

To hear just one of the tracks in SAMPLE.ORC — for instance the Bass track — use the Solo feature.

As you can see from the Track's name in SAMPLE.ORC, Track 2 has been recorded as the Bass line. If you want to hear just that track, use the Solo column.

Soloing a Track

To Play Just the Bass Track:

- Click the S (Solo) column for the Bass track. An "S" displays.
- Now only the Bass line plays as SAMPLE.ORC continues to loop.

Changing a Column's Width

If you can't read all the information in the track Name column, you can adjust the column's width.

To Change the Width of a Column:

- Click the word Name at the top of the column to expand the column.
- Click again and the column width contracts.

To Expand or Shrink All of the Columns at Once:

- Click the double-headed arrow at the top of the Number column.
- A mini-menu opens that lets you Expand or Shrink all of the columns at once.

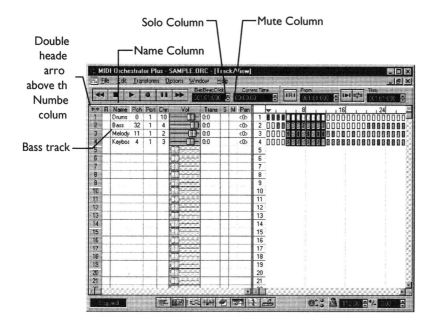

Solo Column — Mute Column

Double heade arro above th Numbe colum

Name Column

Bass track

Muting a Track

Suppose you want to hear all of the tracks **except** one — in this case, the Bass track. In a multitrack recording, you can use Mute to silence as many tracks as you want.

To Mute a Track:

- Un-solo any track(s) you've soloed by clicking the Solo column again.

- Then click the Mute column in the Bass track. The Bass track is muted while the other tracks play.

If you want to Mute all of the tracks except one, it's more convenient to use the Solo feature for that individual track than to Mute numerous tracks!

MIDI Recording

Now that you've loaded and played the sample file, you can use your MIDI keyboard to play along with it and record new tracks — adding to the song as you go. Don't worry about creating a great solo, just play whatever comes to mind!

 Before you begin recording, make certain your system is hooked up correctly. If you are uncertain, refer to the section on MediaCheck in the Appendix of this manual.

To Record a New Track:

1. If you haven't done so already, switch to the Track/View window and load the sample file — SAMPLE.ORC.

2. Click the mouse in the Record column for Track 5. The letter R appears, indicating that recorded data will go to this track.

    • You could have chosen any track without data on it for recording. However, choosing the next available free track makes it easier to display and work on your songs.

3. You're now ready to record MIDI on this track.

4. Click on the Channel column to select a new channel number. This can be done in several ways:

    • By directly typing in the number.

    • By using the spin arrows

    • By pressing the + or - key on the numeric keypad.

    Be sure that the Channel number you select is different from the other Channel numbers listed, otherwise you will be recording with the same Patch (instrument sound) as another channel.

5. Click on the instrument sound you would like to record with.

6. Click the Record button on the Transport Bar. With SAMPLE.ORC loaded, you'll hear a four-beat count-in from the Metronome before recording actually starts. During the count-in, the Transport Status indicator, the box at the far left of the Status Bar, reads "Rec Ready." After the count-in, the display changes to the word "Recording" and recording begins.

7. Play something on your MIDI keyboard. If you don't hear anything, run MediaCheck. (See the Appendix for information about this diagnostic utility.) Otherwise, record to the end of the sample file —or beyond it if you wish. To end the recording, click the Stop button or press the Spacebar on your computer keyboard. The Play Position pointer automatically resets to the beginning of the file.

8. Click the Play button to listen to your recording.

9. In the Name column, enter a name for track 5, the track you just recorded. Do this by clicking the mouse in the column or by using the arrow keys on your computer keyboard to move the Selection rectangle over it and then type in a name.

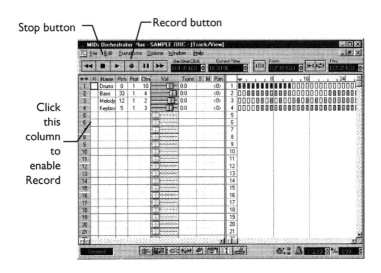

Stop button ─┐   ┌─Record button

Click this column to enable Record

Using Mute and Solo While Recording

You can Mute or Solo tracks during recording in the same way you did during playback.

To illustrate, you might Mute out all tracks and just play along with the Drums track or the Bass line.

Muting the other tracks makes it easier for you to follow the rhythm tracks while you're recording.

Any tracks that you have turned off with the Solo or Mute buttons will be deleted during the Save operation if you save your file in standard MIDI format.

Saving in Voyetra's *.ORC format keeps all Track/View panel settings — including Muted and Soloed tracks.

See "Saving Your Recording" for more information.

Multitrack Recording Techniques

When you record to a track with data on it, MIDI Orchestrator Plus always replaces the existing data with the newly recorded material. Therefore, it's generally a better idea to record new material to new tracks.

In the previous example, "To Record a New Track," you could have recorded the new material to Track 6, leaving the music you recorded on Track 5 undisturbed. Then, during editing, you could merge parts of the two tracks. You'll see how this is done in later chapters.

A good multitrack recording technique is to record multiple "takes" of a given part on different tracks. Each time you record the part, Mute the previous takes. Then cut-and-paste the best parts of the various recordings to assemble your final part.

Saving Your Recording

Do not save your revisions under the filename SAMPLE.ORC. You will need the complete original SAMPLE.ORC file for the tutorials that follow.

You will want to save your recording under a new name without overwriting the original SAMPLE.ORC file.

To Save Your Recording with a New Name:

1. From the File Menu, choose Save As. This opens the File Save dialog box. You'll notice that the File Type at the lower left is set to Orchestrator.

   The .ORC file is MIDI Orchestrator Plus' native file format. .ORC files are, however, proprietary to Voyetra and can only be used by MIDI Orchestrator Plus and other Voyetra programs. To exchange data with programs from other manufacturers, MIDI Orchestrator Plus lets you save your files in standard MIDI (.MID) format.

2. Type in a new name for the file. (Should you want to use the name of an existing file, use the Audition button to listen to that file before overwriting it.)

3. Click OK to save the file under the new name.

Before you save a file in standard MIDI format, check all of your Mute and Solo settings. Any tracks that you have turned off with the Solo or Mute buttons will be deleted during the save operation.

When in doubt, save your file in the .ORC format. This will save all tracks — including those which have been Muted or Soloed. If necessary, you can always re-open the file at a later date and save it in another format.

Closing MIDI Orchestrator Plus

Before closing MIDI Orchestrator Plus, open the Options menu and select Save Settings on Exit.

- A check mark appears to the left of the Save Settings on Exit name when this feature is enabled.

When you use this option, MIDI Orchestrator Plus saves the setup of the editing windows you have opened — including the last four files you worked on — and a number of other configuration settings.

There Are Several Ways to Exit MIDI Orchestrator Plus:

- Double-click on the Control box in the upper left corner of the Main Program Title Bar.
- Click on the Close button in the upper right corner of the Main Program Title Bar (Windows 95).
- Select Exit from the File menu.
- Press the ALT+F4 keys simultaneously.

If you haven't saved the file you're working on, MIDI Orchestrator Plus will prompt you to do so before closing.

If you have been running MIDI Orchestrator Plus with many windows open, you may want to close some before exiting.
With Save Settings on Exit enabled, all the currently open windows will be opened again the next time you start the program. This can drain valuable Windows resource memory.

Learning from the Sample Files

MIDI Orchestrator Plus includes several sample files from Voyetra's MIDI Music Gallery™ collection of song files. These files are located in the demos\midfiles directory.

We suggest that you listen to these files — using the Solo and Mute buttons to isolate parts of their musical arrangements — to gain a sense of how they work.

MIDI Orchestrator Plus also includes many sample drum tracks which you can use as templates on which to build your own songs.

Building a Song

The most common and efficient way to create a MIDI file is to build it in steps, almost as you would a house. You start with the foundation, add a framework, and continue step-by-step until you complete the finishing touches.

Many experienced musicians begin with the drum part. You can create just a few bars of drums then copy and paste them repeatedly, extending a small sample into a longer drum track. Or you can use one of the sample drum tracks provided on the CD-ROM. These are located in the demos\drumtrax directory.

Next, you can play your drum track as you record a bass line, or perhaps a piano, guitar or other rhythm instrument. Once you establish the drums and rhythm, the rest of the song falls into place more easily and creating music is more fun.

With a little practice and the included demo files, you'll be creating incredible-sounding music in no time...and we're certain you'll have lots of fun doing it.

Assigning Tracks and Channels

As you compose a MIDI sequence, you'll need a way to maintain your bearings — to locate and edit musical material as it accumulates in the file. Here are some tips:

Assign each drum instrument to its own track.
> This gives you more complete control and lets you adjust each drum instrument's parameters separately.

One channel (almost always 10 or 16) is set aside exclusively for drums — and that channel works differently from the rest.
> On melodic instrument (non-drum) channels, the key you play determines the pitch of the note and all the notes play the same patch (instrument) sound. Pitch is not a factor for drums, so each individual key triggers a different drum instrument.

Assign each track its own channel.
> If you assign track 1 to channel 1, track 2 to channel 2, and so on, editing and organizing your music will be much easier.

Assign the more crucial instruments (patches) to the lower-numbered channels.
> Every synthesizer has a limited ability to create sounds, so it isn't difficult to create a composition that includes more MIDI data than your synth can play. When this happens, some notes are dropped to make resources available for others. The process, called *voice-stealing*, assigns priority to notes partly according to the channel assignment.

The above tips account for 16 tracks and 16 channels, yet MIDI Orchestrator Plus offers 1000 tracks or more. What do you do with the other 984? The extra tracks can be useful for:

Extra ports and MIDI interfaces.
> Each port can carry 16 channels. Many MIDI interfaces have multiple ports, and a system can have several MIDI interfaces. In the real world, an arrangement of 1,000 tracks would be rare, but, theoretically at least, it's possible. Arrangements of 64 or more tracks are not uncommon.

Cutting-and-pasting.
Empty tracks which won't interfere with finished material are a good place to temporarily store pieces of your composition as you work.

Re-takes.
If you make a mistake while playing a part, re-play it on a new track so you won't lose the previous take. Then, if you wish, you can stitch together the best parts from several takes onto another track.

Harmony.
If your arrangement calls for several of the same instruments playing in harmony, put each part on its own track so you can edit or transpose them independently.

Drums.
Divide drum sounds among several tracks to avoid confusion and to make it easier to manipulate them separately. For example, put the snare drum on one track and the hi-hat on another.

When you have assembled all the pieces you need, copy the finished material onto the first 16 tracks/channels, then Mute or delete the rest. The techniques for all these concepts are discussed later in this manual.

Online Video Tutorials

MIDI Orchestrator Plus is a very powerful program, and there are far more techniques to learn than a single tutorial chapter can cover.

- To help you become acquainted with all of the program's features, we've included three online video tutorials. By now you should have viewed the first tutorial, the MIDI Orchestrator Plus Tour. To learn more about recording and editing in MIDI Orchestrator Plus, view the other two online tutorials.

The Video Tutorial Menu

To view the video tutorials:

1. Put the MIDI Orchestrator Plus disc in the CD-ROM drive.
2. Click the Video Tutorial icon in the Voyetra program group.
3. When the Video Tutorial menu screen displays, click either:

   ❷ Recording in MIDI Orchestrator Plus

   ~ or ~

   ❸ Editing in MIDI Orchestrator Plus
4. Sit back and watch the videos.

Chapter 5

Transport Controls and Status Bar

The Main window in MIDI Orchestrator Plus features two control bars: the Transport Bar and the Status Bar. The Transport and Status Bar controls are available at all times — regardless of which windows are open — and control or give indications about data and settings in the currently active editing window.

Transport Bar

These are the various controls on the Transport bar, just below the Menu bar, near the top of the Main window.

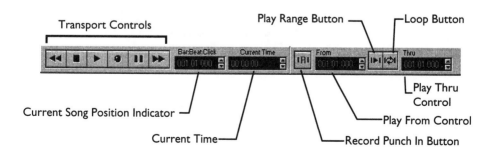

Transport Controls

The Transport controls function in much the same way as the buttons on a tape deck. They enable you to start and stop recording and playback or fast forward or rewind to a desired position within a song.

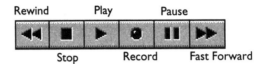

There are two ways to access the Transport controls — either with the mouse or the keyboard.

To Operate the Transport Controls with the Mouse:

1. Place your mouse pointer on the desired button.
2. Click the left mouse button to "press" the Transport control.

To Operate the Transport Controls with the Keyboard:

1. Each Transport control has been assigned a corresponding function key from F4 to F9.
2. Press the function key for the desired Transport control.

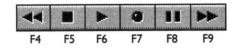

Using the Transport Controls

Rewind (F4)

Clicking and holding the Rewind button moves the pointer backward through the song in small increments.

- To rewind more rapidly, hold the Shift key on the computer keyboard then click and hold down the Rewind button.
- To return to the beginning of the song, double-click the Rewind button.

Stop (F5)

Clicking the Stop button halts playback or recording and automatically rewinds to the position at which playback or recording started.

- To Stop playback or recording using the keyboard, press the Spacebar.

Play (F6)

Clicking the Play button initiates playback of the song, starting from the current position as specified in the Bar:Beat:Click display.

- To Start playback using the keyboard, press the Spacebar.

Record (F7)

Clicking the Record button initiates the recording of new MIDI data onto the record-enabled track. See the section on Record in the "Track/View Window" chapter for details on how to enable a track for recording.

After clicking the Record button, you will hear a count-in interval before recording actually starts. You can set the length of this count-in using the Metronome Settings dialog box. For more information on this dialog, see the "Options Menu" chapter.

During the count-in period, the Record button's red LED blinks and the Status box displays Rec Ready. Once the count-in has finished, MIDI Orchestrator Plus begins recording, as indicated by a solid red LED. The display in the Recording Status box in the Status Bar changes to "Record."

Pause (F8)

Clicking the Pause button temporarily halts playback or recording.

- Once paused, clicking the Pause button again resumes playback or recording without rewinding.

Fast Forward (F9)

Clicking and holding the Fast Forward button moves the pointer forward through the song in small increments.

- To advance more rapidly, hold the Shift key on the computer keyboard then click and hold down the Fast Forward button.
- To advance to the end of the song, double-click the Fast Forward button.

Other Transport Bar Controls

There are several other controls and indicators located in the Transport Bar.

Current Song Position Indicator

 This numerical display shows the current song position in the format Bar:Beat:Click.

The timing resolution (clicks) is set at 480 pulses per quarter note by default. To change the data in this box, use the keyboard or the spin buttons.

When using the keyboard, click on the box, then enter the desired numbers for Bar:Beat:Click in free-form fashion, using any of these symbols ; : , . - as separators.

For example:

4	would be	Bar 4
5-2	would be	Bar 5, Beat 2
2.2.3	would be	Bar 2, Beat 2, Click 3

When using the minus sign (-), be sure NOT to use the minus key on the numeric keypad. The minus sign on the numeric keypad is for reducing the value of the numbers; it does not work as a separator.

The values in this box also can be changed using the spin buttons in conjunction with the Shift and Ctrl keys. See the Appendix on "Changing Numericals" for the different key combinations.

Current Time

This indicator displays the current amount of time elapsed from the beginning of the song.

The Current Time value for a given position in the song will depend on the song's tempo. This information can come in handy when you're creating a song for a time-critical application such as a film, video, or multimedia presentation.

The format in the Current Time box is: Minutes: Seconds: Hundredths.

If you are uncertain of the current settings, rest your mouse pointer on the Current Time box and the Tool Tips help displays the format.

As in the Current Song Position Indicator, you can enter data free-form, from the keyboard, using the symbols   ; : , . - as separators. To do so, click on the box and then enter the desired numbers.

The values in the Current Time box also can be changed by using the spin buttons in conjunction with the Shift and Ctrl keys. See the Appendix on "Changing Numericals" for the different key combinations.

Play From Control

 Use the Play From control to set the starting point of a range within a song file. Play From uses the format Bar:Beat:Click.

In conjunction with the Play Thru control, this control sets a precise range for auditioning, for looping or for recording a file.

As in the other indicators on the Transport bar, you can enter data free-form from the keyboard using the symbols ; : , . - as separators. To do so, click on the box and then enter the desired numbers.

The values in the Play From Control also can be changed by using the spin buttons in conjunction with the Shift and Ctrl keys. Refer to the Appendix on Changing Numericals for the different key combinations.

Play Thru Control

 The Play Thru control sets the ending point of a selected range within a song file in the format Bar:Beat:Click.

In conjunction with the Play From control, this function sets a precise range for auditioning, looping or recording a file.

As in the Play From Control, you can enter data free-form from the keyboard using the symbols ; : , . - as separators. To do so, click on the box and then enter the desired numbers.

The values in the Play Thru Control also can be changed by using the spin buttons in conjunction with the Shift and Ctrl keys. See the

Appendix on "Changing Numericals" for the different key combinations.

Play Range Button

 The Play Range button plays the range of measures set in the Play From and Play Thru controls.

Loop Button

 The Loop button plays and repeats the range of the file as set in the Play From and Play Thru controls.

To Loop a Selected Range:

1. In any window, select the portion of the file you wish to loop. This can be done by:
   - Clicking-and-dragging over the portion you would like to select. Once you've selected the area, Ctrl-click in the From and Thru boxes to enter the Start and End times of the selected range.
   - Entering the start and end times in the From and Thru controls by clicking the spin buttons or by typing in the Start and End times.
   - Clicking-and-dragging in the Ruler Bar area, over the area you wish to select. Then Ctrl-click in the From and Thru boxes to enter the Start and End times of the selected range.
2. Click the Loop Range button. The selected range plays repeatedly until you click the Stop button or press the Spacebar.

Record Punch In Button

 Clicking the Punch In button toggles between normal recording mode and *Punch In* recording mode.

Punch In recording mode allows you to record a specific region of the song. This region is defined by the Bar:Beat:Click values in the From/Thru controls.

Set the range you want, click the Record Punch In button, and then the Record button. Recording of the new music begins at the time you've set in the From indicator, ends with the time in the Thru indicator, and then stops automatically. For additional information about recording, see the "Track/View" chapter.

To Record a Range:

1. Set the range to record using the From and Thru controls.
2. Click the R column to enable a track for recording.
3. Click the Record Punch In button.
4. Click the Record button. You will hear a lead-in passage consisting of a number of bars of music in your song leading up to the beginning of the selected range. You can set the number of bars in the lead-in using the Metronome Settings command in the Options menu.
5. Record the new music. The recording will stop automatically at the end of the selected range.

 To learn more about recording in MIDI Orchestrator Plus, watch the online tutorial on Recording.
  1. Put the disc in the CD-ROM drive.
  2. Click the Video Tutorial icon in the Voyetra program group
  3. Click ❷ Recording in MIDI Orchestrator Plus.
  4. Sit back and watch the video.

Punch In Recording

Very often, you may want to begin recording from a certain point in the song. This is called Punch In recording. For example, if you recorded up to a certain point in the song and then made a mistake, you could go back and "punch in" record where the mistake was made. Punch In recording records only the bars that you specify — in this case, the bad part — and leaves the good section alone.

To Record from the Middle of a Song (Punch In Recording):

1. Click File on the Menu Bar and open SAMPLE.ORC.

   - If you have loaded it recently, click its name on the list of most recently accessed files at the bottom of the drop-down menu list.

   - If it is currently loaded, click No when prompted to save the copy of SAMPLE.ORC that's now loaded. (This restores the original version of SAMPLE.ORC without any changes.)

2. Now we want to set the From and Thru controls to the range from bar 8 to bar 40. One way to do this is to click the From and Thru controls and then type in the numbers.

3. With the Range selected, click the Record Punch In button on the Transport Bar. The button turns black when it is activated.

   - With Record Punch In activated, recording begins after the Intro and ends just before the 2-bar ending phrase of the song.

   - When you record using the Punch In feature, Record count-in works differently. MIDI Orchestrator Plus plays a number of bars before the selected range to cue you in to start recording. Recording begins when the Play Position Pointer enters the range you've selected, in this case, bar 8.

   - By default, the number of lead-in bars is one. If you want a longer lead-in, you can change this value in the Metronome Settings dialog box. Open this dialog by clicking the Options menu and selecting Metronome Settings.

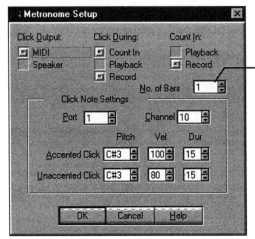

Increase or decrease the Count In by changing the value in the No. of Bars box.

Metronome Setup Dialog Box

4. For our first Punch In recording, let's use a 4-bar Count In. Click the up arrow in the No. of Bars box to change the setting to 4. Click OK to close the dialog box.

5. Now you can begin recording by clicking the Record button on the Transport Bar. You don't have to click Stop; MIDI Orchestrator Plus automatically stops recording when you reach the end of the selected range.

6. Click the Play button to listen to the new recording. If you don't like what you hear, click Undo in the Edit menu and try again.

7. When you're happy with your recording, save your song under the filename "MYFIRST.ORC."

 Do NOT save your file as SAMPLE.ORC! You'll want to keep the SAMPLE.ORC file unchanged, so that you can use it in other tutorials!

Status Bar

Like the Transport Bar, the Status Bar at the bottom of the Main window is available at all times.

Status Bar indicators and controls are tied to the data in the currently-active editing window.

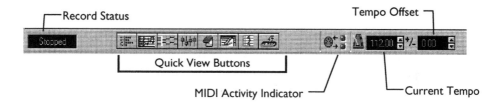

Record Status

This indicator displays the current status of the transport:

- Stopped
- Playing
- Paused
- Rec Ready
- Recording

Quick View Buttons

The fastest way to open sub-windows in MIDI Orchestrator Plus is with the Quick View buttons. These are located at the bottom of the Main window. There is one Quick View button for each of the editing windows in MIDI Orchestrator Plus. A single click on any button quickly displays the desired window.

Track/   Piano   Note-   Con-
View   Roll   pad   ductor
                        Editor

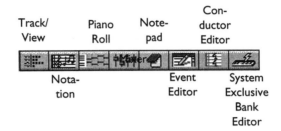

Nota-   Event   System
tion   Editor   Exclusive
                                Bank
                                Editor

Quick View buttons CANNOT be used to open multiple instances of an editing window. Use the New command in the Window menu to open additional views of an editing window.

When more than one editing window is open, pressing the Ctrl+Tab keys together enables you to jump from window to window.

MIDI Activity Indicator

 The MIDI Activity Indicator contains two LEDs: the top one shows MIDI input, the bottom one shows MIDI output, as indicated by the in and out arrows.

When recording, the input indicator flashes green to show that valid MIDI data is being received by MIDI Orchestrator Plus.

The output indicator flashes green when MIDI data is being transmitted by MIDI Orchestrator Plus.

The LEDs flash red if invalid MIDI data is received.

Current Tempo

 The Current Tempo control displays the current tempo of a MIDI song with a resolution of 1/100th of a beat per minute.

Set tempo to any value between 16 and 500 beats per minute by:

- Using the spin buttons.
- Clicking on the numerical panel and typing in a value.
- Pressing Ctrl+T and then using the + and - keys on numeric keypad.

Tempo Offset

 The Tempo Offset control displays the amount by which a MIDI song's tempo will be increased or decreased in beats per minute.

Like Current Tempo, Tempo Offset is calibrated to a resolution of 1/100th of a beat per minute.

Set the tempo offset to any value between -100.00 and 100.00 by:

- Using the spin buttons.
- Clicking on the box and entering a value.

Setting Tempo Offset

Whenever you change the tempo in a song, you are actually sending a MIDI message that establishes a new tempo. Any tempo change message sets a value that remains in effect until another tempo change occurs — or until the end of the song. Most MIDI files contain at least one tempo change message, and often more. Together, these messages form a *tempo map* for the song.

The Tempo offset changes all the tempos in the tempo map by the amount specified. For example, if a song's tempo map is 120, 125, then 131 and you set the tempo offset to +10, the new tempo map will be 130, 135, and 141.

If you save the song as a standard .MID file, the offset will be incorporated into the tempo map. In MIDI Orchestrator Plus' .ORC file format, the tempo and tempo offset are saved as independent values.

Tempo maps let you incorporate tempo changes into a musical composition to speed up or slow down the tempo. You can use a series of small tempo changes to construct gradual increases or decreases in tempo known as *accelerandos* and *ritardandos*. Tempos, time signatures, and key changes are treated as separate events and are assembled in the Conductor track. These are discussed in the chapter on the "Conductor Editor."

Chapter 6

Track/View Window

The Track/View window is MIDI Orchestrator Plus' default window and opens automatically when you first run the program.

There are several ways to open the Track/View window:

- Click the Track/View window Quick View button at the bottom of the screen.
- Select New and then Track/View from the Window menu.

 You can open only one instance of the Track/View window.

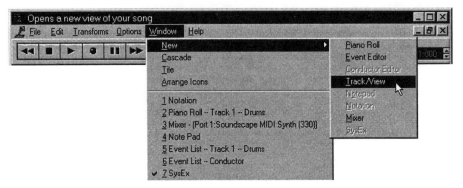

Opening the Track/View Window
from the Window Menu

Quick Tour

Track/View is the window you will use most often. This window provides a "track sheet" that condenses a large amount of information into a small area— showing you all the MIDI data in your song in a single view.

In addition to using the mouse, you can also use the arrow keys, the PgUp and PgDn keys or the scroll bars to move around within the Track pane. You can use the Tab key to move between the Track and Bar panes.

Most of the columns in Track/View have spin buttons to facilitate changing values. Up and Down spin arrows appear when you click the column. You can use the "+" and "-" keys on the numerical keypad or the mouse to change these values.

For the Name, Patch, Port and Volume columns, clicking the column heading toggles between expanded and reduced width views. Clicking the double-headed arrow in the column above the track numbers expands all of these columns at once.

By clicking-and-dragging on the name of a column, you can rearrange the order in which the columns appear in the Track pane.

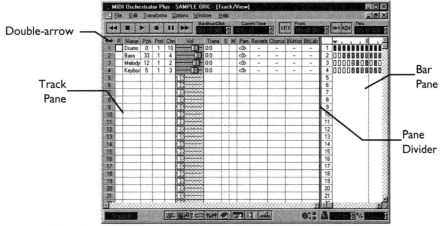

Double-arrow

Track Pane

Bar Pane

Pane Divider

The Track/View window is divided into two separate sections or panes — the Track pane and the Bar pane. The Pane Divider — the vertical border between the two panes — can be dragged left or right with the mouse, to resize the panes.

Track Pane

Expand/Shrink All

Expand All
Shrink All
Bar View

Clicking the double-arrow button at the upper left of the Track pane pops up a menu that allows you to quickly re-size the Track/View window to one of three configurations:

Expand All — maximizes the Track pane with all adjustable columns set to expanded width.

Shrink All — minimizes each column in the Track pane; all adjustable columns are set to the reduced width display.

Bar View — maximizes the Bar pane, completely hiding the Track pane.

↔	R	Name	Vol	Patch	Port	Chn
1		Drums	▭▭	Drums	2	10
2		Bass	▭	Acoustic Bass	1	4
3		Melody	▭	Vibraphone	1	2
4		Keyboard	▭▭	Electric Piano 1	2	3
5						
6						
7						
8						
9						
10						
11						
12						
13						
14						
15						
16						
17						
18						
19						
20						

Track/View window
showing Shrink and Expand settings.

Track Number

In the column beneath the double-headed arrow, a number for each track is displayed. There are a total of 1,000 tracks available.

You can move any track by clicking on its track number box and dragging it up or down to the desired location. Once you drop the track in its new location, the other tracks are shifted down and renumbered.

You can delete any track by clicking-and-holding on its track number box and pressing the Delete key.

If you move or delete a track accidentally, pull-down the Edit menu and click Undo.

Record Enable (R)

 Click in the "R" column to enable a track for recording. A red "R" appears in that column. The track that displays the "R" show that any recorded material will be sent to that selected track. Clicking a second time toggles off Record Enable.

For multitrack recording, you can enable more than one track at a time by Ctrl-clicking in the Record Enable column. (To Ctrl-click, hold down the Ctrl key while clicking the left mouse button.) Using multiple tracks for recording allows you to record on multiple MIDI channels simultaneously.

Name

 This column displays a name for each track. Click the Name box to enter the desired text or edit the existing name.

Click the heading to toggle between expanded and reduced width for this column.

Patch (Pch)

 This column displays the patch — the sound that you want the track to use — as either a patch number (when the column is in reduced width) or a patch name (when the column is in expanded width).

Patches are numbered from 0-127.

The Patch parameter setting causes the specified patch to be called up for that track every time you start playback.

Click the right mouse button to bring up the Patch Selection dialog box which shows all of the available patch names.

The default, Patch Map is General MIDI, but you can change the selection in the Patch Map Setup dialog. See the chapter on the "Options Menu" for full details.

The Patch Selection dialog box uses the General MIDI Patch Map by default — but you can set up your own by selecting Patch Map Setup from the Options menu.

Port

This column displays the MIDI output port — or device — to which the track is assigned. The Port column displays either a port number (when the column is in reduced width) or a name (when the column is in expanded width).

Right-clicking the Port column brings up the Port Selection dialog box, which provides a complete listing of all port selections.

If you have a multi-port MIDI setup, this can make it easier to switch between ports and drivers.

For example, if you have a MIDI interface that has 2-In/2-Out capabilities, you can set up different MIDI devices for your MIDI Out. You might have a General MIDI synth on one output port (port 1) and an a dedicated piano sound module on the other (port 2).

You can make sure that your piano tracks go to the better piano module by setting each of those tracks to output port 2.

Click the heading of this column to toggle between expanded and reduced width display.

Volume (Vol.)

 This column shows a track's MIDI Volume setting as either a numerical value between 1 and 128 (when the column is in reduced width) or a horizontal slider (when the column is in expanded width).

You can click the heading of this column to toggle between the expanded and reduced width displays.

The Volume parameter will transmit a MIDI Volume message on the specified channel whenever you start playback or change this setting. The Velocity On value can also affect the volume of a note, so if you increase the value in the Velocity Offset column you will also increase the volume on playback.

Channel (Chn)

This column shows the MIDI channel (1-16) to which the MIDI events in a track will be routed. Each different instrumental patch (sound) you use in your music needs to be set to a different channel.

You can change the channel assignment for a track by clicking this column and typing in a new value or by using the spin buttons to cycle through the channels available.

For each output port you have defined in your port setup you will have 16 channels to choose from. This makes it possible to have very complexly orchestrated arrangements with more than 16 channels.

Don't forget that in General MIDI, Channel 10 is reserved for percussion. For a complete listing of the "General MIDI Patch Set," refer to the Appendix at the back of this book.

Transpose (Trans)

Trans
0:0
0:0
0:0
0:1 v

This column contains the track's transposition setting in the format Octaves:Semitones, with an arrow indicating whether the track is being transposed up or down.

You can transpose a track up or down by as much as 10:7, ten octaves and a fifth.

To Transpose down, use negative numbers. To Transpose up, use positive numbers. So, for example:

-2   transposes down two octaves
1,1   transposes up one octave and one semitone

Pressing the + or - keys on the numeric keypad will increase or decrease the Transpose parameter by one semitone, respectively. For example, 1:0^ is up one octave, 0:7^ is up a perfect fifth, etc. You can use the spin buttons for changing these settings.

Solo (S)

 This column displays the track's Solo status. When a track is Soloed, as indicated by an "S" in the Solo box, all other tracks are muted.

You click a track's Solo box to toggle Solo on or off. If you hold down the Ctrl key and click, you can Solo more than one track at a time.

Mute (M)

 This displays the track's Mute status. When a track is muted — as indicated by an "M" in the Mute box — it will not trigger any notes or transmit any other type of MIDI data.

Click a track's Mute box to toggle Mute on or off. You can Mute multiple tracks, if desired.

Pan

The Pan settings affect the relative left and right volume settings for stereo playback.

This column contains the track's left/right pan positioning as a numerical value with an arrow indicating left or right panning.

Negative numbers are interpreted as pan left. Positive numbers are interpreted as pan right.

Pan values are defined as:

$$<64 \ = \ \text{full left}$$
$$<0> \ = \ \text{center}$$
$$63> \ = \ \text{full right}$$

The Pan setting transmits a MIDI Pan message on the specified channel whenever you start playback or change its value. The MIDI Standard sets the left and right to be unequal values.

Controller A and Controller B

These two controls let you set a value between 1 and 128 for two different MIDI Controllers such as Reverb or Chorus. The controls send a MIDI Controller message on the specified channel whenever you start playback or change the controller value.

If your sound card or MIDI device doesn't support the selected MIDI Controller, the parameter has no effect.

The name or number of the assigned MIDI Controller appears in the title box at the top of the column after you have assigned it in the Controllers dialog box.

Clicking this control pops up spin buttons to facilitate cycling through the range of controller numbers.

Note that like volume, changing the Controller setting does not affect the underlying MIDI data but only sets up a MIDI Controller event that globally affects the way the song sounds on playback.

For a list of "General MIDI Controller Types," refer to the Appendix at the back of this book.

Bank Select High & Low, (BkMsb - BkLsb)

BkMsb	BkLsb
--	--
127	--
0	1
--	--

The MIDI standard supports up to 16,384 banks of 128 different instrument sounds, or "patches." Some keyboards and sound cards will respond to Bank Select messages that allow you to access sets of patches stored in their memory.

If your keyboard or sound card supports this feature, you can use the BkMsb (Most Significant Byte) and BkLsb (Least Significant Byte) columns to send such messages to your device. Refer to your keyboard's manual for meaningful numbers.

Left-clicking this control brings up spin buttons for quickly changing the patch number. Right-clicking causes the Patch Selection dialog box to display, allowing you to select a patch by name.

Bar Pane

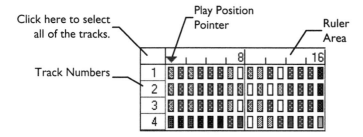

Click here to select all of the tracks.

Play Position Pointer

Ruler Area

Track Numbers

The Bar pane displays the measures — or bars — that make up each track of MIDI. At the top of the Bar pane is a scale — the Ruler Area — which indicates the bar numbers. The Play Position Pointer, a red triangle, shows the current location within the song.

When displaying MIDI tracks, the Bar pane consists of rows of boxes. Each row of boxes represents the bars in a particular track. The shading of each box represents the relative density of notes and other MIDI events within that bar. A white box contains no MIDI events but it may contain the tail end of notes from the previous measure.

To move around within the Bar pane, you can use the mouse, the arrow keys, the PgUp and PgDn keys or the scroll bars.

In the Bar pane, if you:

- Double-click on a MIDI track, the Piano Roll window will appear and display the track.
- Ctrl+double-click on the MIDI track, the Event List window will appear and display the track.
- Click on a Track number, the entire track will be selected.
- Click in the area just above the Track numbers, all of the tracks will be selected.
- Pull down the Edit menu and click on Select All (or use the key combination CTRL+A), all of the tracks will be selected.
- Press the left mouse button as you move the mouse across the Ruler Area, all of the tracks in the measures you have moved the mouse across will be selected.

To move the Play Position pointer, position the mouse arrow at the desired location in the Ruler Area and click the right mouse button.

Cutting, Copying, and Pasting

The techniques for cutting, copying and pasting data in MIDI Orchestrator Plus are similar to the techniques used in word processing.

Cutting Data

You can select areas and events, highlight them by dragging the mouse over them and then cut them to the Clipboard using the Cut command in the Edit menu.

When you Cut data, the selected region is removed from the location of the cut and stored in MIDI Orchestrator Plus' Clipboard. An interval of silence equal to the data which has been cut replaces it.

Cut data can be pasted at another location in the window, into another instance of the window, into a different MIDI Orchestrator Plus window or even into a different .ORC or .MID file.

Keyboard Shortcut Key: Ctrl+X

To Cut Data Using the Cut Command:

1. Load the SAMPLE.ORC file and switch to the Track/View.
2. Highlight some MIDI data.
3. Choose the Cut command from the Edit menu. This copies the data into the MIDI Orchestrator Plus Clipboard.
4. When you close the file, do NOT save it with the changes!

 After you have cut, copied or pasted data in the sample file, DO NOT save the file as SAMPLE.ORC! You'll want to keep the SAMPLE.ORC file unchanged, so that you can use it in other tutorials!

Copying MIDI Tracks

The Copy command works similarly to Cut; however, in Copy, no interval of silence replaces the selected data. Here, a copy of the selected data is moved to MIDI Orchestrator Plus' Clipboard, while the original data remains behind.

Keyboard Shortcut Key: Ctrl+C

To Copy Data Using the Copy Command:

1. Load the SAMPLE.ORC file and switch to the Track/View.
2. Highlight some MIDI data.
3. Choose the Copy command from the Edit menu. This copies the data into the MIDI Orchestrator Plus Clipboard.
4. Close the file without saving it!

Pasting Data from the Clipboard

Once you have either cut or copied data to MIDI Orchestrator Plus' internal Clipboard you can paste it into a new location using the Paste command in the Edit menu.

*   If you put the data into the Clipboard by dragging it, then you paste it simply by dropping it at the new location. Refer to "Using Drag-and-Drop" later in this chapter.
*   If you want the data you're pasting to replace the data at the site of the paste, select the data at the site before pasting.
*   If you want the data you're pasting to merge with data at the site of the paste, rather than selecting the data at the site of the paste, place the cursor at the beginning of the range you wish to merge into, then paste.

To Paste Data in the Track/View Window:

1. Use the Cut or Copy techniques previously described to place the selected data in the Clipboard.

2. Select a range beginning at the point where you wish to place the contents of the Clipboard. When you use the Paste command, MIDI Orchestrator Plus replaces the data you selected at the site of the paste with the data in the Clipboard.

3. If you want the data to merge with the existing material, do not select any data at the area of the paste. Instead, click the mouse at the point where you want the data to be pasted.

4. Choose Paste from the Edit menu to paste the data.

   • If you selected a range in the previous step, the contents of the Clipboard will replace any existing data, beginning at the starting point of that range.

   • If you did not select a range, the data will merge, beginning at the point where you clicked the mouse.

 To delete the contents of the Clipboard and any Undo information, use the Clear Clipboard command on the Edit menu.

But be careful — this action CANNOT be undone! Once the contents of the Clipboard have been cleared, this information is gone forever!

Using Drag-and-Drop

If you want the data on the Clipboard to merge with the data at the site of the paste, or if you're pasting data to the end of a track, you can use the drag-and-drop method:

1. Select a range with the mouse.
2. Place the cursor anywhere in the range.
3. Drag the data to the new location.
4. An interval of silence replaces the data you dragged to the new location.
   - If you prefer to leave a copy of the data behind, hold down the Ctrl key as you drag.
5. Release the mouse button. The data is pasted into the new location, beginning at the cursor position. Unless you are pasting data at the end of a track, the data you drop will merge with the existing data.

Cutting vs. Deleting Bars

These two commands in the Edit menu — Cut Bars and Delete Bars — both remove data from a file, but there are important differences in the way each works.

Cutting Bars

Cut removes the notes from the selected area and leaves empty measures behind. The data is placed in the Clipboard, allowing you to paste it into another location if you wish.

Deleting Bars

Delete Bars removes both the notes and the measures. The Delete Bars command does not place the deleted material in the Clipboard nor does

does it leave empty measures behind. Instead it shifts subsequent measures to the left to fill in the gap left by the deleted material.

You can also delete bars by placing the cursor at the desired start location and choosing the Delete Bars command from the Edit menu. From the dialog box, you can select the range of bars to be deleted. If you choose a single track in the Delete Bars dialog box, data is removed only from that track.

Inserting Bars

You can insert any number of blank bars in the middle of a song by calling up the Insert Bars dialog box from the Edit menu. If you want data to move ahead in time when you're pasting material in, you can use Insert Bars to create empty measures and then merge the data into those measures. In this way, you can add data to the middle of a song without really merging it with the existing data or replacing the existing data. This is something you can't do using traditional Cut, Copy and Paste methods.

Chapter 7

Notation Window

The Notation window lets you transcribe, view and print tracks as standard musical notation. It incorporates a number of sophisticated features, including rest suppression, quantization options, selectable clef and split point and variable zoom.

The Notation window gives you very fast and accurate staff printouts that you can use to copyright or distribute your songs. If you want to edit the transcription, you must edit the underlying MIDI data from another window, such as Piano Roll.

There are several ways to open the Notation window:

- Click the Notation Quick View button.
- Select New and then Notation from the Window menu.

 You can open only one instance of the Notation window.

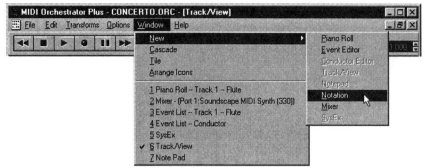

*Opening the Notation Window
from the Window Menu.*

Quick Tour

Let's take a look at the Notation window.

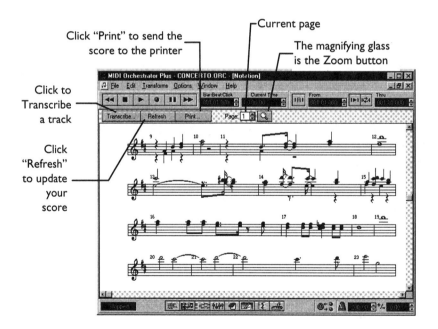

Use the Current Page control or the scroll bars to move around within the Notation window.

During playback, the current bar is indicated by a red pointer. This allows you to follow along in the Notation window as a song plays.

Notation Window Toolbar

The Notation window has its own Toolbar with the following controls:

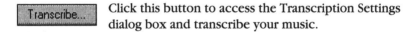

Transcribe

 Click this button to access the Transcription Settings dialog box and transcribe your music.

This dialog box gives you complete options on how you want your musical score to appear. It's covered in detail later in this chapter.

Refresh

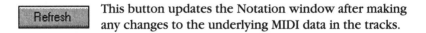 This button updates the Notation window after making any changes to the underlying MIDI data in the tracks.

The Refresh button is unavailable unless you've made changes to the track.

Print

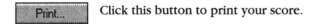 Click this button to print your score.

Page

 This control allows you to move between pages.

Zoom

 Clicking this button opens the Notation Zoom menu.

You can choose one of the pre-set values or choose "X%" to open the Zoom Percentage dialog box and set any value from 10% to 200%.

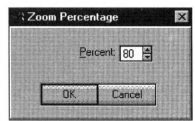

Zoom Percentage Dialog Box

Changing the magnification of the screen image enables you to see how the whole page will look when printed or to check the details of particular parts of your score.

- A good general-purpose setting is usually 70%.
- A setting of 35% will allow you to view an entire page of your score at a glance.

Quick Start Printing

If you want to test the transcribing and printing functions quickly, use the following procedures to get a fast printout.

To Open the Notation Window:

1. If you're working in a different editing window, click the Notation Quick View button (2nd from the left) at the bottom of the screen.

2. The Notation window opens on a blank screen since you haven't yet transcribed any tracks into it.

3. To display music in the Notation window, click the Transcribe button. The Transcription Settings dialog box displays, giving you access to a number of parameters, but, for now, just click in the Show column for Track 1 and then click the OK button.

4. After a brief pause, a staff and notes appear on the screen.

To Print Your Score:

1. Click the Transcribe button.

2. In the Transcription settings dialog box, enter the name of the song in the Title dialog box.

3. Select the Track or Tracks that contain the parts you want to print and enter any other information, if applicable, in the appropriate box.

4. Leave the rest of the settings at their defaults and click OK.

5. Click the Print button. Make any necessary adjustments for your printer. Then click OK.

6. Check the resulting printout. You may want to adjust the Notation parameters to produce a more refined score.

 If you're experiencing any problems printing your score, open Windows Font Manager and make sure the MIDI Orchestrator Plus notation font, SPW.TTF, is loaded. This font was installed with MIDI Orchestrator Plus, but changes to your system may have affected Windows font loading. If this True Type font is not installed, reinstall it from the MIDI Orchestrator Plus CD-ROM, just as you would install any True Type font.

Transcription Settings Dialog Box

MIDI Orchestrator Plus gets its transcription parameters from the entries in this box. The Transcription Settings dialog box lets you select the track(s) you want to transcribe and configure a number of other settings.

The order in which the selected tracks open from top to bottom in the window is how they will appear in the notation. If you want a different order, reorder the tracks in the Track/View by pulling on the Track Number in the Track Pane and dragging it to the desired location.

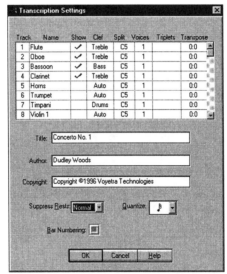

Transcription Settings dialog box

Track

This column shows the number for each of the tracks in the song.

Name

This column displays the track name for each track.

Show

This column selects the track(s) you want to transcribe into notation.

When you click the column, a check mark appears to show the track is being transcribed.

Clef

The clef box allows you to select the clef into which your music will be transcribed. When set at the default —Auto — MIDI Orchestrator Plus determines the best clef for transcription.

Alternately, you can choose from one of five available clef options: Treble, Bass, Alto, Tenor and Grand Staff. You'll use Treble, Bass and Grand Staff (Treble and Bass clefs) most often.

Split

This column displays the split point — as a note name and octave number — where the Grand Staff splits the bass and treble clefs.

If you have music with a wide range that should be displayed in a Grand Staff, you'll need to choose a split point.

The split point is the note value that determines the staff in which the notes will appear. For example, using a Grand Staff and setting a split point of C5 (Middle C) means that any notes below Middle C will appear in the bass clef, while Middle C itself and any notes higher will appear in the treble clef. If Grand Staff or Auto is not the selected clef, the split point values will be ignored.

Voices

In many piano and orchestral pieces, you'll find more than one musical idea occurring at the same time. There might be two flutes playing imitative music, but they're both recorded to the same track. This can be expressed in notation by including more than one "voice" per musical staff.

MIDI Orchestrator Plus allows you to choose between one-voice transcription and two-voice transcription for each track. The voice with upward stems would represent one musical idea and the voice with downward stems would represent another. If you create music with this level of complexity, you'll appreciate this feature.

Triplets

If your music contains triplets, three notes played in the space of two, activate the triplet-sensing feature by clicking this column. With the Triplets icon displayed, the number "3" will appear in the score over the appropriate notes.

Combining triplet-sensing with the correct quantization and rest suppression values will yield a more accurate musical score.

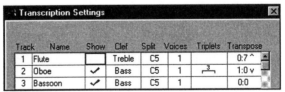

Track	Name	Show	Clef	Split	Voices	Triplets	Transpose
1	Flute		Treble	C5	1		0:7 ^
2	Oboe	✓	Bass	C5	1	3	1:0 v
3	Bassoon	✓	Bass	C5	1		0:0

The Triplets feature is activated for Track 2.

Note that the Triplets feature only works with eighth note triplets.

Transpose

 Transposing music notation track by track is crucial when printing out parts for transposing instruments — that is, instruments that are not pitched in C.

When you create a score in MIDI, you are working in concert pitch and assuming that every instrument produces a Middle C when the score calls for it. However, this is not the case.

Imagine a score which uses strings, timpani, trumpet and alto saxophone. If you ask a trumpet player to play Middle C, you'll actually hear a B-flat. This is because the trumpet is pitched in B-flat. To hear a Middle C, you'll need to print a score where everything is raised a Major second. Additionally, you would transpose the alto sax part up a Major sixth because it is keyed in E-flat. The strings and timpani would not need transposition.

 The Transpose function affects the way the music is notated only — not the MIDI data itself.

Title

Title: Concerto No. 1

Use this box to insert a title at the top of the score.

Author

Type your name — or the composer's name — in this box.

Copyright

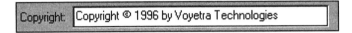

Type the copyright and the date in this box. Use ALT-0169 to print the © character. If needed, use the Windows Character Map utility to enter other non-standard characters.

Suppress Rests

The Suppress Rests options give you control over how silences will be notated in your music.

In many cases, if you let MIDI Orchestrator Plus notate the rests exactly to the level of quantization you've set, you'll find your score littered with lots of very small rest values.

In order to clean the appearance of your score, you can add one of two levels of rest suppression:

Normal Extends note values over rests with small durations, thereby eliminating the rest.

Fill Also suppresses rests, but goes further than Normal by filling note durations all the way to the beat as represented by the time signature in the music.

Off Disables rest suppression.

Quantize

The Quantize control lets you set the level of quantization for the transcription of your score.

Quantize does not affect your MIDI data at all, it merely cleans and tightens up the look of the score.

To Quantize MIDI Data:

- Begin by choosing the smallest significant rhythmic value you want notated, from quarter notes through sixty-fourth notes, and select that value from the control.
- When you click the Transcribe button again, all note start times and lengths are shifted and lengthened to the nearest multiple of the selected quantization value.

MIDI Orchestrator Plus rounds-off the start times and durations of all notes to the nearest multiple of the selected Quantize value.

Transcription settings do not quantize or otherwise change the actual notes in the song file; they only affect the display of notes in the Notation window.

Bar Numbering

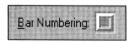

Toggles bar numbering On or Off. The Bar Numbering button lets you choose whether or not to include small bar numbers in your score.

When bar numbering is selected, a small bar number is displayed above each measure along the topmost staff of your score.

Fine Tuning Notation

Getting a computer to capture and display musical notation in an accurate and readable way can be a formidable task. The difficulty arises when you try to get the computer to convert a musical performance full of human "feel" directly into notation from a MIDI file.

Using the Quantize function can help, but too coarse a quantization value may not represent the source file accurately. However, too fine a quantization value can make the score impossible to read, cluttering the staff with an over-abundance of notes and rests.

The trick is to find a balance between representing the performance precisely and making the score look good. Quantization only solves part of this problem, but we can use another MIDI Orchestrator Plus tool: Suppress Rests.

In the same way that quantization pulls a note to the nearest quantize level, rest suppression looks at a note's duration and decides when a note should be scored with a duration longer than actually played. This is where rest suppression comes in.

- If you turn Suppress Rests off, it will put a rest after every note you played a little too short.
- With rest suppression set to Fill, the notes are lengthened, the rests are hidden and the score becomes much more readable.
- To allow some rests to be displayed, choose the Normal setting. This will give you a compromise between Off and Fill.

Chapter 8

Piano Roll Window

The Piano Roll window lets you work with MIDI data note-by-note. Using the mouse to move and resize the notes that appear in the editing window, you can add or delete notes and change their duration and pitch. You can sound the notes one at a time or continuously as you move the mouse across the screen.

You can open a second pane at the bottom of the Piano Roll window displaying each track of your song in standard musical notation. This score is updated each time you make a change in the editing window.

There are several ways to open the Piano Roll window:

- Double-click any MIDI bar in the Bar Pane of the Track/View window; this opens the Piano Roll window at the bar position you clicked.
- Click the Piano Roll Quick View button in the Status bar.
- To open multiple instances of the Piano Roll window, select New and then Piano Roll from the Window menu.

Opening the Piano Roll window
from the Window menu.

Quick Tour

The Piano Roll window has its own Toolbar where the editing tools and most of the indicators and controls are located. The window can be split vertically into Piano Roll and Notation Panes.

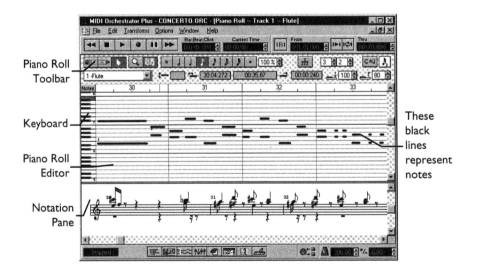

Piano Roll Toolbar

Keyboard

Piano Roll Editor

Notation Pane

These black lines represent notes

Right-Click Menu

Clicking the right mouse button anywhere in the Piano Roll opens a menu from which editing tools can be selected or other operations can be performed.

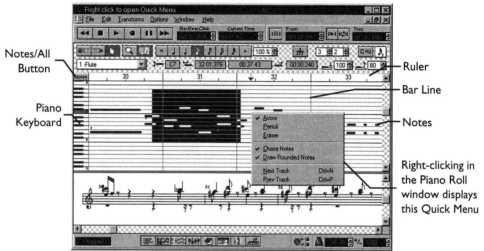

Notes/All Button

Piano Keyboard

Ruler

Bar Line

Notes

Right-clicking in the Piano Roll window displays this Quick Menu

Right-clicking anywhere in the editing window opens the Piano Roll Quick Menu displayed here.

Musical Data in the Piano Roll Window

Here is how musical data is represented in the Piano Roll window.

- Notes in the editing window are represented as thin rectangles.
- The length of these rectangles corresponds to their duration.
- The vertical axis represents pitch.
- The horizontal axis represents time.
- A ruler at the top of the editing area indicates the bar numbers and the beat divisions within each bar.
- Bars are separated by a vertical line.

- The graphical piano keyboard at the left edge of the window shows the pitch and octave number for the note to its right.

Features of the Piano Roll Window

In the Piano Roll window, you can quickly edit the pitch, start time or duration of existing notes, as well as move or copy notes.

- The graphical piano keyboard works just like a miniature piano keyboard. You can play notes simply by clicking on the keys.
- To highlight a series of measures, click and hold the left mouse button and move the mouse horizontally across the Ruler area.
- To highlight a series of notes, click and hold the left mouse button and move the mouse vertically across the piano keys on the left side of the window.
- To select all of the tracks in the entire song, use the Select All command on the Edit pull-down menu or press Ctrl+A.
- To "scrub" (play) any of the notes recorded on the Piano Roll, click-and-hold the *right* mouse button in the Ruler area at the top of the window and drag the cursor line over the notes.

Notes/All Button

Clicking the Notes/All button, located just above the graphical piano keyboard, toggles edit mode between All MIDI data and Notes only. When in Notes mode, only notes will be affected when editing. When in All mode, all MIDI data will be affected — including MIDI controllers, benders, modulation, etc.

- To cut a note at the same point where a MIDI program change is embedded, but you want to keep the program change, select Notes mode.
- To delete the program change and any other MIDI data at that point in the bar, select All mode.

Piano Roll Toolbar

The Piano Roll Toolbar is located just beneath the Transport Controls.

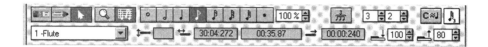

Pencil

 When you select this tool, the cursor changes to a pencil shape.

The Pencil tool lets you insert new notes by clicking at the desired location in the editing area.

- Clicking inserts and plays a note with the current Insert Note parameters.
- Double-clicking displays the Event Edit dialog box from which you can select the parameters for the note you're inserting.
- Clicking-and-dragging enables you to draw any length note with the Pencil.

Eraser

 When you select this tool, the cursor changes to an eraser shape. The Eraser tool deletes notes.

Any note you click on with the Eraser tool will be deleted.

- Clicking individual notes erases single notes one-at-a-time.
- Clicking-and-dragging the Eraser tool over an area erases a series of notes quickly.

Arrow

 When you select this tool, the cursor changes to the normal arrow shape. The Arrow is the default editing tool.

Use the Arrow Tool To:

- Graphically edit the Start Time, Pitch or Duration of existing notes by clicking and dragging.
- Edit an existing note by double-clicking on it and adjusting its parameters in the Event Edit dialog box.
- Insert new notes by double-clicking at the desired location in the editing area. The note will play when inserted.
- Highlight an area to be edited by Cut, Copy, or any of the Transforms commands.
- Click the right mouse button to play the piano keys without highlighting.
- Select the location at which notes will be pasted with the Paste command.
- Click any existing note causing the note to "sound" and verify its pitch.
- "Scrub" notes, making them sound, by clicking-and-holding the right mouse button in the Ruler Bar area and dragging the cursor line over the notes.
- Audition notes with the arrow by clicking the left mouse button in the piano keyboard area and dragging to highlight. This causes each musical half-step to sound as you move the arrow.

 These three tools — the Pencil, Eraser and Arrow — also can be selected from the Piano Roll Quick Menu. To access this menu, click the right mouse button anywhere in the Piano Roll window.

Note Duration Buttons

 If you want to insert notes in the track, begin by choosing how long the notes will last.

The Note duration buttons show notes from a whole note to a sixty-fourth note.

- Click one of these buttons to select the Duration for the note you're inserting.
- Enable the Dotted Note button to add a dot to the selected note duration.
- A dot increases a note's duration by 50%.

Articulation

 The Articulation feature allows you to vary the Duration of the Insert Note between 10% and 110%.

An articulation value greater than 100% will cause adjacent notes to overlap. Although most MIDI devices respond correctly to overlapping notes some do not, so check your documentation if you encounter problems at high Articulation settings.

- Use a lower articulation setting in situations where a shorter (*staccato*) playing style is needed.
- Use a higher articulation setting where a smooth, connected (*legato*) style is desirable.

Tuplet Controls

Used in conjunction with the Duration buttons, the Tuplets feature lets you specify a non-standard Duration for the Insert Note, such as a tuplet, triplet or quintuplet.

Tuplets On/Off

 When the Tuplets control is on, all Insert Notes are given the duration as if they were a tuplet. Set this button to On only when you are inserting multiple tuplets.

Tuplet Numerator and Denominator

This control displays the Tuplets ratio which is defined as x notes in the space of y durations.

For example, if you wanted to insert a quarter note triplet, you would select a quarter note Duration, enable Tuplets and set the Tuplets ratio to 3:2. This would allow you to insert three quarter notes (a triplet) in the space normally taken by two quarter notes.

In order to insert evenly spaced tuplets it's a good idea to set the grid to the same value as the tuplets you are planning to insert.

Snap-to-Grid

The Piano Roll window includes a Grid feature that allows for easier, more precise placement of inserted or edited notes. The Grid feature automatically rounds off or *quantizes* the Start Times of inserted notes, and Start Time and Durations of edited notes, to the nearest interval on an imaginary grid.

The Grid treats inserted notes differently from notes that already exist. When you insert a new note, any Grid setup will only affect the starting position of the note. The duration of the note is determined by the note type and the value entered for its Articulation.

When editing this same note, however, different rules apply.

- Dragging the entire note will keep its duration, but snap its new starting position to a Grid interval.
- Adjusting its duration will snap the duration to a Grid interval.

Snap On/Off

 This button toggles the Grid feature on and off. When the Grid is on, the selected notes are pulled — or *snapped* — to the grid lines.

Snap Value

 Snap Value displays the selected value for the snap feature and, therefore, the interval of the Grid.

You can set the value from a quarter note through a sixty-fourth note triplet by repeatedly clicking this button.

A Snap Value of an eighth note, for example, will cause the Start Time and Duration of any edited notes to snap to one of eight grid points in a 4/4 bar. A Grid interval of an eighth note triplet will cause the Start Time and Duration of any edited note to snap to one of 12 grid points in a 4/4 bar (three triplets per beat, multiplied by four beats in a measure).

Track

 This control displays the track name and number. Click this control to jump to any other track.

Insert Pitch

 This control displays the current position of the cursor in the editing area — or the pitch of the note being edited. The information is represented as a note name and octave number.

Insert Point in Bar:Beat:Click

`33:01:285` This control displays the current position of the cursor in the editing area or the Start Time of the note being edited in the format Bar:Beat:Click.

Insert Point in Minutes:Seconds:Hundredths

`00:38.57` This control displays the current position of the cursor in the editing area or the Start Time of the note being edited in the format Minutes:Seconds:Hundredths.

Insert Length

`00:00:090` This control displays the Duration of the Insert Note or the note being edited in the format Bars:Beats:Clicks.

On Vel

 This control displays the MIDI On Velocity of the Insert Note.

Off Vel

 This control displays the MIDI Off Velocity of the Insert Note.

Zoom Control

 Use the Zoom control to select one of several different windows for editing. When you click the Zoom button, the following menu selections become available:

Range Zooms in on a range you've selected in the editing area. Use this setting for precise editing of a specific area.

User Switches to a user-defined zoom setting which has been saved with the Save User command.

Default Is a good general-purpose setting for most editing tasks.

Max Out Zooms all the way out to view the largest possible area.

Save User Saves the current window as the User window.

Notation On/Off

 This command toggles the Notation pane on and off. The button darkens when Notation is selected.

With the Notation pane open, the current track is transcribed and displayed in a pane at the bottom of the Piano Roll window.

This lets you view notes in Piano Roll format and as conventional music notation at the same time. Any changes or edits executed in the Piano Roll pane will be immediately reflected in the Notation pane. See the section on the "Notation Pane" later in this chapter for more information on this feature.

Changing Numerical Values

To change the values in boxes which accept numerical data, you can use the spin buttons alone or in conjunction with the Shift and Ctrl keys. For more information about changing numerical values, see the Appendix titled "Changing Numerical Values."

Piano Roll Quick Menu

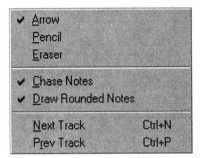

Clicking the right mouse button any-where in the Piano Roll window pops up a Quick Menu with several of the same items which appear on the Piano Roll Toolbar.

For a more detailed explanation of the Arrow, Pencil and Eraser, refer to the sections on these icons earlier in this chapter.

Chase Notes

This option allows you to configure the editing area so that notes which start to the left of the display will extend into the editing area if necessary.

When scrolling backwards and forwards through measures in the Piano Roll, you will find that some notes that cross bar lines will not appear until you are looking at the measure where the note begins. If this is a problem, you can turn on Chase Notes. This tells MIDI Orchestrator Plus to graphically display any notes that are being held across from a previous measure into the measure that you are viewing.

Because of the convenience of this feature, chances are you'll want Chase Notes set to On all the time. Once you've selected it, Chase Notes will stay on if you have checked "Save Settings on Exit" in the Options menu.

When Save Settings on Exit in the Options menu is checked, MIDI Orchestrator Plus saves the current screen and configuration settings when you close the program. These are then restored the next time you open the program. If you have many windows open, you may want to close some before exiting.

Rounded Notes

When this option is enabled, notes will be displayed with rounded corners.

- Rounded corners make it easier to see the meeting point between two adjacent notes.
- Square corners make it easier to see precisely where a note begins and ends.

Next Track/Prev Track

These commands allow you to easily switch to the next or previous track.

Use the following Keyboard Shortcut Keys to jump to the Next and Previous tracks in the Piano Roll window:

Ctrl+N   jumps to the Next track

Ctrl+P   jumps to the Previous track

Notation Pane

Right-clicking anywhere within the Notation pane displays the Piano Roll's Transcription Settings dialog box. This dialog lets you control the way that notation will appear. See the "Notation Window" chapter for additional information.

Although you can see your song in standard musical notation in the Notation pane, you cannot edit the notes here. All note-by-note editing is done in the Piano Roll pane. However, any changes you make to the notes are instantly reflected in the Notation pane.

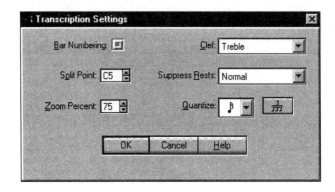

Bar Numbering	Toggles bar numbering On or Off. When On, the number of each bar is printed along the topmost staff.
Split Point	Displays the split point for the bass and treble clefs in a Grand Staff. The split point is shown as a note name and octave number. Notes at or above this pitch will be placed in the treble clef; notes below this pitch will be placed in the bass clef.
Zoom Percent	Lets you set the size at which notation will appear on the screen.
Clef	Lets you choose the clef in which the notation appears. Selecting Auto tells MIDI Orchestrator Plus to determine the best clef for notating the MIDI data.
Suppress Rests	Choose one of three values telling MIDI Orchestrator Plus how to display rests: Off, Normal and Fill.
Quantize	Choose the level of quantization for the displayed score. This does not affect the MIDI data, only the displayed notation.
Enable Triplets	Toggles triplets On or Off. When On, the number "3" appears in the notation over the appropriate notes.

For additional information on these features, refer to the "Notation" chapter.

Chapter 9

Mixer Window

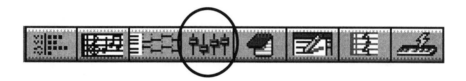

The Mixer window gives you a quick and easy way to balance volumes and try out patch and controller settings. The window has the appearance of a "mixing console" with sliders and knobs for adjusting settings like volume, pan, solo and mute for each of the 16 channels on a single MIDI port. Each port can have its own mixer of 16 channels.

There are several ways to open the Mixer window:

- Click the Mixer Quick View button at the bottom of the screen.
- To open multiple instances of the Mixer window, select New and then Mixer from the Window menu.

*Opening the Mixer Window
from the Window menu.*

Quick Tour

The Mixer window's graphical interface can make it easier to identify and orchestrate the individual parts of your song.

Right-click in this area to display MIDI Output Port settings

Volume Slider

Clicking the right mouse button in the right side of the Mixer window displays the different MIDI Output Ports available on your system.

Using the Mixer

The Mixer window is used to:

- Create an optimum mix by fine-tuning the relative volumes of the instruments.
- Audition different sounds (patches) for a particular part.
- Optimize an existing song file for playback on your sound card or MIDI setup.
- Adjust controller settings such as reverb and chorus.
- The Track/View and Mixer windows share many of the same controls and methods. When you change a setting in one window, both will change.

Channel Info

Click here
to open the
Channel
Info Dialog
box

By clicking on a channel module's Info button, you can access its Channel Info dialog box.

Channel Info Dialog Box

The following settings can be displayed and changed from the Channel Info dialog box:

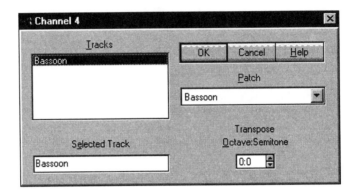

Tracks on Channel

This lists the names of all the tracks assigned to the MIDI channel for the selected channel module. From here you can select tracks for naming or transposing.

Since any single channel can have more than one track assigned to it, you can use this box to check channel assignments for your mixer settings. Click on a track to select it.

Selected Tracks

You can edit the track name in this box. The new track name will appear in the Tk Name area at the bottom of the window when you click OK to close the Channel Info dialog. It becomes the new name for the track throughout the application appearing in all MIDI Orchestrator Plus windows and lists.

Patch

Choose any of the 128 available MIDI patches for the selected track in this list box. For more information on Patches see the "Track/View" chapter.

For a listing of the 128 instruments in the "General MIDI Patch Set," refer to the Appendix of this manual.

Transpose

This lets you transpose (change key) on a selected track by semitones or octaves. For example, 1:0^ is equal to going up one octave, 0:7^ is up a perfect fifth, etc.

For more details on transposing see the "Track/View" chapter.

MIDI Density Meters

MIDI density meters

As a song plays, the MIDI density meters blink to show which channels are active. The number of LEDs lit gives a relative indication of how much MIDI data is being played on the track.

Controller A and Controller B Settings

Just above the row of Solo buttons are two rows of knobs labeled Chorus and Reverb and, further down, another row labeled Pan. These knobs operate MIDI controllers — non-note MIDI messages that affect the operation of your synthesizer.

 For a listing of General MIDI Controller Types, refer to the Appendix at the back of this book.

Controllers —

By selecting Controllers from the Options menu, you can re-assign the two controller knobs so they'll operate the MIDI controllers you use most frequently. When you re-assign a controller knob, the appropriate label appears to the right of the knob.

Note that the Pan knob is permanently assigned to the Pan Controller 10 and cannot be reassigned.

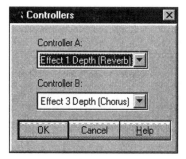

If your sound card or MIDI device does not support the selected MIDI Controller, this parameter will have no effect.

Controller A defaults to Reverb, Controller B defaults to Chorus.

Solo

The Solo buttons let you Solo a particular MIDI channel, which silences all the other channels. When a channel is Soloed, its LED will be lit.

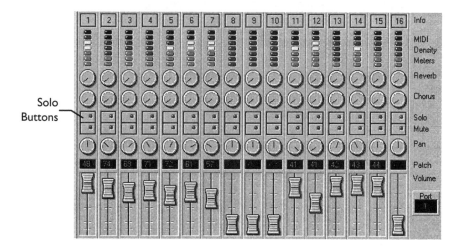

In the Mixer window, you can also Solo a group of channels by Ctrl-clicking on the Solo buttons for each of the desired channel modules.

There are many situations where it's helpful to concentrate on a single part of your arrangement and to temporarily silence the rest. To Solo a track, click its Solo button. All the other channels become silent.

Notice that the LED indicators always tell you which of the buttons is active.

Mute

The Mute buttons let you mute (silence) or un-mute a particular MIDI channel on playback without affecting the underlying data.

When a channel is muted, the Mute LED will be lit.

Mute Buttons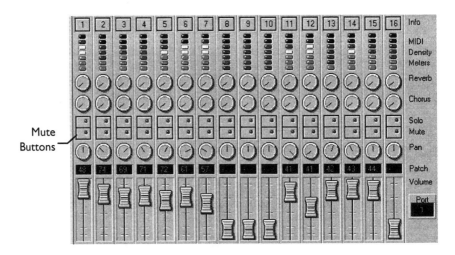

- To mute (silence) a channel, click its Mute button.
- Click the Mute button again to turn the sound back on.

You can mute as many channels at a time as you wish.

 If you want to Mute all tracks except one, it's more convenient to use the Solo feature for that individual track than to Mute numerous tracks!

Pan

Used for stereo playback, the Pan control sets the channel's left/right positioning.

Turn the knob to the left or right with your mouse to set that channel in the stereo field.

Pan
Knobs
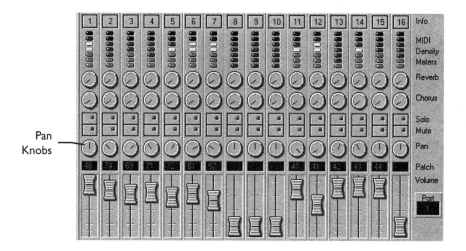

The Pan parameter will transmit a MIDI Pan message on the specified channel whenever you start playback or change its value.

If your sound card or MIDI device doesn't support MIDI Pan — or you're playing back through a mono sound system — this parameter will have no effect.

Patch Selector

This control lets you select an instrument sound for each channel. The ability to control patches is one of the most valuable aspects of MIDI synthesis.

Patch
Selector
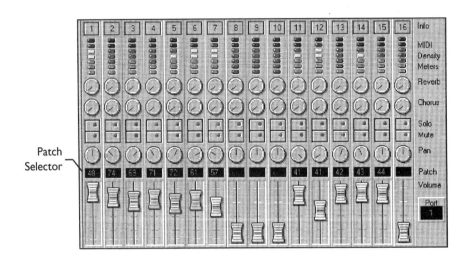

To Change the Patch Assignment:

- Click the patch selector. The number increases if you click the top half of the window and decreases if you click the bottom half.

You should hear a change in one of the instruments as you change the patch. Change the patch a few more times and try it on some of the other channels (other than 10 or 16).

Volume Sliders

These sliders let you adjust the volume of each channel so you can create a "mix" for your song, just as you would on an external mixing console.

Volume Sliders

You can drag the volume sliders up or down with the mouse to raise or lower the playback volume of each channel independently. Experimenting with changes of volume as your song plays can help you to find a mix that you like.

Port

The Port control allows you to select the output port that you wish to control with the Mixer window. The Title Bar tells you which Port is active. Each Port controls 16 MIDI channels, one per module in the Mixer window. Clicking the right mouse button in the right side of the Mixer window displays the MIDI Output Port box.

The information displayed on your screen
will be specific to your system and may differ
from what appears here.

Track Name

This display shows a track name for each channel. If more than one track is assigned to a channel, Tk Name displays the name of the first track assigned to the channel according to track number.

Track
Name

*Due to the size of the display,
long track names will only show
the first few letters of the name.*

By clicking on the module's Info button, you can select a different track name to be displayed here or change the name of any of the tracks assigned to the channel.

Switching momentarily to the Track/View screen can give you a quick overview of track and channel assignments.

Chapter 10

Notepad

The Notepad is a handy place to store such text-based information as a file's name, author and copyright, tempo or other song settings, song lyrics or any comments you want to have on hand when you're working with a song.

You can enter text in MIDI Orchestrator Plus' Notepad the same way you do in Windows. The difference is that the text is added to and saved along with your song file.

There are several ways to open the Notepad window:

- Click the Notepad Quick View button at the bottom of the screen.
- Select New and then Notepad from the Window menu.

 You can open only one instance of the Notepad.

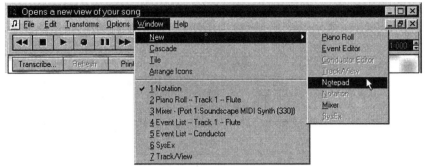

*Opening the Notepad Window
from the Window menu.*

Quick Tour

Use the Notepad to cut, copy and paste text between MIDI Orchestrator Plus and other Windows applications. When you save your song as an .ORC or .MID file, anything you've typed into the Notepad window will be saved along with it. The next time you open the file, you can open the Notepad window to review your comments.

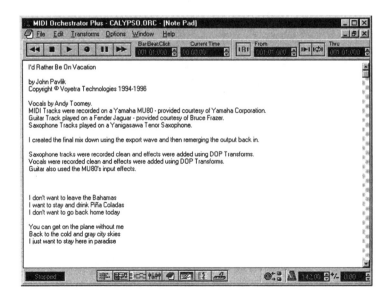

Chapter 11

Event Editor

The Event Editor displays MIDI data from a single track in the form a sequential list of individual MIDI events. These can be *note events*, with information about start, velocity, pitch and duration, or *non-note events*, containing data such as MIDI Controller, Pitch Bend or Patch Change messages.

There are several ways to open the Event Editor window:

- Click the Event Editor Quick View button at the bottom of the screen.
- To open multiple instances of the Event Editor, select New and then Event Editor from the Window menu.

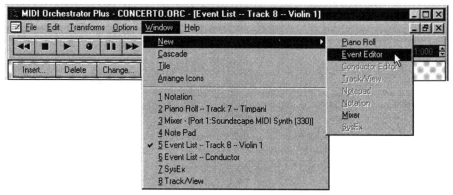

*Opening the Event Editor
from the Window menu.*

Quick Tour

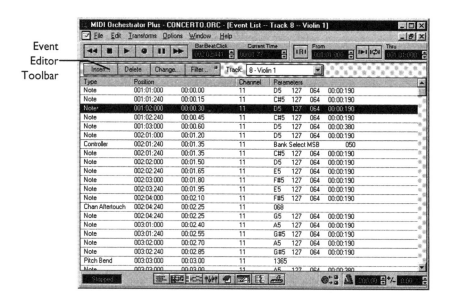

Event
Editor
Toolbar

The Event editing window shows MIDI data as a series of note and
non-note events. Each event can be edited individually.

Unlike most displays in MIDI Orchestrator Plus, which use a left-to-right orientation to indicate time, the Event Editor window's Event List is arranged vertically. Earlier events are nearer the top of the list.

Using the Event List, you can edit any kind of event including notes, patches, pitch wheel, aftertouch, velocities and controllers on a micro-level.

Each row in the Event Editor represents a specific MIDI event.

- The first column tells you the Type of event.
- The second column gives you the Position of that event in the song.
- The third column gives the Channel assignment.
- The fourth column lists the Parameters that control the event.

As you play through a song, the list scrolls from top to bottom and the Highlight moves to show the event currently being played.

To Use the Event Editor:

1. Select Open from the File menu to load a .MID or .ORC file.
2. Open the Event Editor by clicking its Quick View button in the Status Bar.
3. Click Play on the Transport Bar to begin playing the file. As the file plays, you'll see a Highlight bar sliding down the page very quickly. This highlight shows every event as it occurs.
4. You can stop the Highlight at a particular event and select it by clicking the Pause button on the Transport Bar as that event occurs.
5. In addition to using the mouse, you can move forward or backward in the Event List by using the vertical scroll bar's up or down arrows or by pressing the PgUp or PgDn keys. You can jump to a different track (including the Conductor track) at any time by clicking on the Track select box in Event Editor's toolbar.

Use the following Keyboard Shortcut Keys to jump to the Next and Previous tracks in the Event Editor window:
Ctrl+N jumps to the Next track
Ctrl+P jumps to the Previous track

Event Editor Toolbar

The Even Editor Toolbar is located at the top of the Event Editor window, just below the Transport Controls.

Selecting a Track

The Track Selection list box on the Event Editor toolbar lets you select any of the tracks in your song.

Once you select a track, the Event Editor fills with the list of the events in that track.

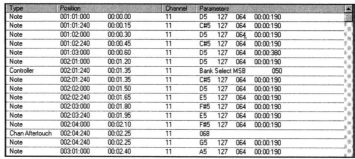

When you first open the Event Editor window,
you'll see the events for the currently selected track —
that is, the one you were last working with.

If the Event Editor opens with a blank list, you most likely activated the window with a track that contains no MIDI data. Use the Track Select box to the right of the Filter button to switch to a different track.

You'll notice that the first track shown in the Track Selection list box is the Conductor Track. This track contains Tempo, Meter, and Key Signature events for the entire song which are separated from the other types of events.

You can open the Event Edit dialog box in Conductor mode by selecting this track in the Event Editor. You can also open the Conductor Editor window by clicking on the Quick View button or by clicking New in the Window menu and then clicking Conductor Editor in the flyout menu. Refer to the "Conductor Editor" chapter for more information on working with this feature.

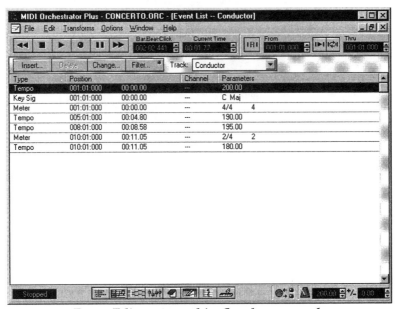

Event Editor opened in Conductor mode.

Inserting a New Event

Before inserting MIDI events in your score, you have to position the highlight at the location where you want the insertion to occur.

To Insert a New Event:

1. Select the appropriate track from the track selector, then play the file to locate the insertion point in Bar:Beat:Click. This can be done by playing the file and clicking Pause to stop it at or near the insertion point.

2. Click the Insert button. The Event Edit dialog box displays.

*Event Edit dialog box
with the Note Event selected*

3. If the Start value of the note is not the same in Bar:Beat:Click as the insertion point you want, you can change this setting in the dialog box and the event will be inserted in precisely the right location.

4. At the left edge of the Event Edit dialog is a window from which you can select the type of event to insert. Select the Note icon if it isn't already selected.

5. Use the parameter boxes to the right to set the other note parameters — Pitch, Velocity and Duration. See the section on the Event Edit dialog box later in this chapter for details on how to set these parameters.

6. Click OK. The new event will be entered at the selected location with the values listed in the Insert dialog box.

Copying and Pasting in the Event List

Events can be moved around in the Event List using the Edit menu's Cut, Copy and Paste commands.

To cut or copy an event or group of events, you must first highlight the data by clicking-and-dragging the mouse. Once the events are highlighted, you can choose the desired command from the Edit menu.

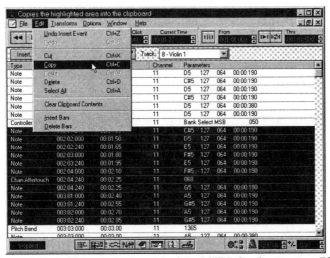

Selected Note Events are copied to MIDI Orchestrator Plus' internal Clipboard using the Edit menu.

Once events have been cut or copied to the edit buffer, you can paste them to a new location by placing the cursor at the desired location and choosing the Paste command from the Edit menu. The Paste Where? dialog box appears, from which you can select the exact location for pasting.

The Paste Where? dialog box lets you choose the exact location of the paste and whether or not you want to overwrite the events at that location.

To delete the contents of the Clipboard and any Undo information, use the Clear Clipboard command on the Edit menu.

But be careful — this action CANNOT be undone! Once the contents of the Clipboard have been cleared, this information is gone forever!

Deleting Events

Unlike the Cut command, the Delete button does not place the deleted events in the edit buffer, so you cannot paste an event back after you have deleted it. You can, however, undo a delete with the Undo command in the Edit menu.

To Delete an Event:

1. Select and highlight the row displaying the event.
2. click the Delete button on the Event Editor toolbar.

If you prefer, you can delete an event by highlighting it and pressing the Delete key on your keyboard.

Changing Events

There are several ways to change an event in a score:

- Select the event. Click the Change button on the toolbar. This brings up the Event Edit dialog box.
- You can also bring up the Event Edit dialog box by double-clicking on the row for the event or highlighting the row and pressing the Enter key on your keyboard.

The Event Edit Dialog Box

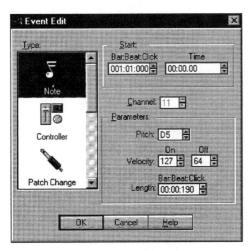

There are seven main types of events that you can edit or insert in MIDI Orchestrator Plus:

- Note
- Controller
- Patch Change, Key
- Aftertouch
- Pitch Bend
- Channel Aftertouch
- SysEx

These events are shown at the left side of the Event Edit dialog box.

If you're editing an existing event and you open the Event Edit dialog box by clicking the Change button, the dialog will open with the event type highlighted.

You can change the parameters for the event but you cannot change the event *type* for an existing event.

If, on the other hand, you are inserting a new event, click on the Insert button to open the Event Edit dialog box. Here you can select which type of event you are going to insert by clicking one of the events in the list at the left of the box.

As you click the different events, the parameters that appear in the right portion of the dialog box change. Every MIDI event has different parameters that control what you hear, and these parameters change depending upon what type of event you are editing or inserting.

Changing an Event's Starting Position

You can change any event's starting position or choose the correct starting position for a new event by editing the Start entry in the Event Edit dialog box.

This entry, or field, is measured in both Bar:Beat:Click and Time.

When you open the Event Edit dialog box to change an event, the Start field displays the current song position of that event.

When you open the dialog to insert a new event, the Start field shows the song position of the last event highlighted, so you may need to edit this value to set the correct insertion point.

Setting the Channel Assignment

This is a display of the channel assignment of a particular event. If you've set a MIDI channel in the Track/View window, all events in the track will be forced to that channel, regardless of the settings that appear in the Event Edit dialog box. To allow an event's unique channel setting to prevail, switch to the Track/View window and set the track's channel to "-" (no channel).

Setting Parameters in the Event Edit Dialog Box

For each event, the Event Edit dialog box contains editable listings for that event's parameter settings. The following parameters can be set for each of the events:

Parameters for Note Events

Pitch   The note's pitch as a note name and octave number (C5 equals Middle C).

Velocity   The note's Note On and Note Off velocities.

Length   The note's duration expressed in Bar:Beat:Click

Parameters for Controller Events

Type   A drop down list of the 128 MIDI Controller types; select the type of controller event you'd like to add.

Value   The numerical value of the controller event (from 0 to 127). For a listing of "General MIDI Controller Types," refer to the Appendix at the back of this book.

Parameters for Patch Change Events

The MIDI standard supports up to 16,384 banks of 128 different instrument sounds, or "patches." Some keyboards and sound cards will respond to Bank Select messages that allow you to access different sets of patches stored in their memory.

If your keyboard or sound card supports this feature, you can use the BkMsb (Most Significant Byte) and BkLsb (Least Significant Byte) columns in Track/View to send your device such messages.

Patch   The patch number.

Bank MSB   The high bank number for use with multi-bank synths.

Bank LSB   The low bank number for use with multi-bank synths.

Name   The name corresponding to the selected patch number; click this button to show the illustrated patch selection dialog box.

If you're not sure whether there's a patch map available for your MIDI device, see the "Options Menu" chapter for information.

Parameters for Key Aftertouch

Note   The note number that the aftertouch will affect.

Value   The amount of aftertouch (from 0 to 127).

Parameter for Pitch Bend

Bend Value   The amount of pitch bend that is applied to notes in a track at a given song position on a scale from -8192 to 8191. This value can also be set from the slider.

Parameter for Channel Aftertouch

Value   The numerical value of the aftertouch event (from 0 to 127).

Parameter for SysEx

Bank   The name of the bank, synth, or device to which the SysEx message is sent. SysEx messages can be edited in the SysEx window.

Summary

This table summarizes the parameters for MIDI events:

Event Type	Parameters
Note	Pitch, On and Off Velocity, Duration
Controller	Controller Name or Number, Value
Patch Change	Patch Name or Number
Key Aftertouch	Pitch, Pressure Amount Value
Pitch Bend	Value
Channel Aftertouch	Pressure Amount Value
SysEx	Bulk Hex Data

 Since not all synthesizers support all Controller messages, you may not be able to hear some of the edits you make.

For additional information, refer to the manual for your synthesizer.

Embedding Patch Changes

Embedding a patch change lets you change instrument sounds at any point in a song automatically. For example, you can change an electric bass sound to a fretless bass sound on a single track and channel at a specified point in a song. Embedding a patch event can make better use of the channels you have by letting you use the same channel to call up different patches. This can be handy if you have used up the available channels in your composition.

Check your synth or sound card's manual to determine which patches are available and what their numbers are. If you have a GM compatible device, the General MIDI names are already listed in the parameter box.

To Embed a Patch Change:

1. Click the Insert button.
2. Click the Patch Change icon.
3. Enter the location where you want the event inserted in Bar:Beat:Click or Time.
4. Open the patch list and highlight a patch. Click OK.

A new patch change event appears in the list at the position you selected. Now, when you play the file from the beginning, you will hear the patch change to the new instrument when it encounters the embedded patch change event.

Inserting (embedding) a patch in the Event list overrides the patch shown in the Track/View. The patch displayed in the Track/View plays from the beginning of the song and remains in effect until the embedded patch comes along again.

If you don't want to use the Track/View patch, leave the Patch Parameter box, in Track/View, blank.

The patches you can select will depend on the sound card or module you are using. If you are using a GM (General MIDI) card or module, MIDI Orchestrator Plus uses the GM patches automatically.

If you have another type of sound device, MIDI Orchestrator Plus can be configured to load its patch map, assuming one is available. You can also create your own Patch Maps. Refer to the VSEQINI.WRI file for full information.

Filtering Events

Locating or editing certain kinds of events can be difficult if they are mixed together with many other events of different types. The event filter limits the items displayed in the list; you see only those events you want to find or change. The filter affects only the display of events in the list. All events, whether filtered or not, remain in the file.

For example, if you want to remove all pitch bends from a track, you could filter everything but pitch bend, then cut the pitch bend messages.

Clicking the Filter button brings up the Filter Events dialog box. The LED on the Filter button will be lit when any event is being filtered.

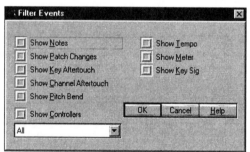

Clicking an item in this dialog box
toggles the display of information
for that item On and Off.

 If the Event Editor shows a blank list and you are certain the track contains data, check the Filter Box to be sure you haven't inadvertently filtered out all the data in the track.

To Delete, Cut or Copy Filtered Events:

1. Click the Filter button. Turn off all the Event buttons **except** the button of the event you wish to edit. Click OK.

2. To select one or more events for editing, click an event or click-and-drag to highlight the desired events.

3. Click the Delete button or use cut/copy/paste commands.

You can refine the filtering even further for MIDI controller events by limiting the display to a single controller type. For example, you might want to "thin out" excessive volume changes (controller 7), mod wheel (controller 1) or other controller messages.

To Filter Controller Types:

1. Click the Filter button. Turn off all Event buttons except the Controller button.

2. Click the Controller drop-down box and select the controller type you wish to edit. Click OK.

3. Edit or delete the desired events.

Editing the Conductor Track from the Event Editor

When you create a new song, MIDI Orchestrator Plus automatically sets it to a default Time Signature (4/4), Tempo (120 bpm) and Key Signature (C Major) by inserting the appropriate events at the very beginning of the Conductor track. You can change the song's initial settings as needed by selecting the Conductor track and opening the Event Edit dialog box.

For information on Conductor settings see the chapter on the "Conductor Editor."

Chapter 12

Conductor Editor

When you click the Conductor Quick View button, you instantly jump to the Conductor Editor window with the Conductor track selected. The Conductor track is a special track that contains the song's Meter, Tempo and Key Signature events.

There are several ways to open the Conductor Editor window:

- Click the Conductor Editor Quick View button at the bottom of the screen.
- Select New and then Conductor Editor from the Window menu. You can open only one instance of the Conductor Editor.

 You can open only one instance of the Conductor Editor window.

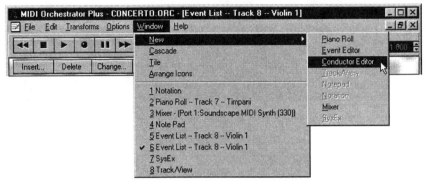

Opening the Conductor Editor
from the Window menu.

Quick Tour

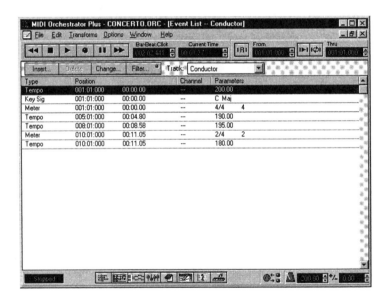

There are three types of events that can be edited in the Conductor Editor: Tempo, Meter, and Key Signature.

The Conductor track contains the Time Signature, Tempo and Key Signature settings for your song. You can include additional events by entering them at different Bar:Beat:Click settings.

When you create a new song, MIDI Orchestrator Plus automatically sets the following defaults by inserting these events at the very beginning of the Conductor track:

- Time Signature (4/4)
- Tempo (120 beats per minute)
- Key Signature (C Major)

You can change the song's initial settings by selecting the Conductor track and editing these events in the Event Editor window.

 Initial events can be edited — but not deleted — from the song

Conductor Editor Toolbar

To Open the Conductor Editor Event Edit Dialog Box:

- Click Insert or Change in the Conductor Editor Toolbar

    ~ or ~

- Double-click an event.

There are actually three different dialog boxes available here — one for each type of event — Tempo, Meter and Key Signature. All three dialog boxes have a similar appearance.

The controls for the Conductor Editor window are the same as those for the Event Editor window. See the chapter on the "Event Editor Window" for additional information.

Tempo Settings

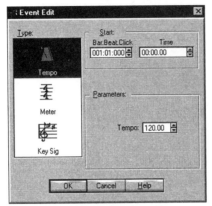

Event Edit Dialog Box —
for Tempo

To Insert Tempo Changes in a File:

1. In the Conductor Editor window, click the Insert button to display the Insert dialog box for Tempo, Meter and Key.

2. Click the Tempo icon, select a new tempo value and Start location in Bar:Beat:Click or Time.

3. Click OK.

The Tempo selection in the Conductor Event Edit dialog box displays the following settings for Tempo events.

Start   Displays the Tempo event's position in both Bar:Beat:Click and Time

Tempo   The tempo in beats per minute from 16 to 500 with a resolution of 1/100th beat per minute.

You will see the new Tempo Change Event inserted in the Event List. You can insert these tempo changes anywhere you would like within the song.

Tempo Maps

Tempo maps let you incorporate tempo changes to speed up or slow down the tempo. You can use a series of small tempo changes to construct gradual *accelerandos* and *ritardandos*.

Meter Settings

Event Edit Dialog Box — for Meter

The Meter setting in the Conductor Event Edit dialog box shows the following settings for your music's time signature:

Start   Displays the start time in Bar:Beat:Click and Time and values for the Numerator, Denominator and Clicks per Bar set for the song.

Numerator   The Numerator is the number of beats a measure contains.

Denominator   The Denominator is the note value of these beats. (For example, 2 = half notes; 4 = quarter notes; 8 = eighth notes; etc.).

Clicks per Bar   Clicks per Bar determines the number of metronome clicks per bar as well as the number of division lines per bar in the scale at the top of the Piano Roll window. This value must divide evenly into the numerator value.

       For example: the time signature is 3/4, set the Numerator to 3, the Denominator to 4, and the Clicks per Bar to either 3 (if you want to hear each beat) or 1 (if the tempo is very fast and you only want to hear each full measure clicking by).

When you change the first Meter setting in the Event Edit dialog box, the values for the entire song are changed. You can insert any number of new time signatures using the Insert button.

Key Signature Settings

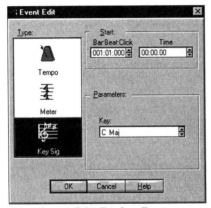

Event Edit Dialog Box —
for Key Signature Settings

Start   Displays the Start time in Bar:Beat:Click and Time for any key changes you make to the song.

Key   Shows the value for the Key Signature, as a key name. In MIDI Orchestrator Plus, the Key Signature affects the way tracks are displayed in the Notation window.

Refer to the chapter on "Notation" for additional information.

Filtering Events

Filtering events in the Conductor Editor works in exactly the same way as in the Event Editor window.

Refer to the "Event Editor" chapter for additional information.

Chapter 13

System Exclusive Bank Editor

System Exclusive (SysEx) messages contain information about patch settings, MIDI configuration, parameters and special settings. However, not all synths use SysEx, so consult your hardware documentation before using this feature.

There are several ways to Open the SysEx window:

- Click the Quick View button at the bottom of the screen.
- Select New and then SysEx from the Window menu.

 You can open only one instance of the System Exclusive Bank Editor window.

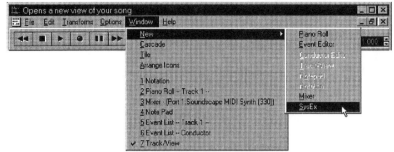

Opening the SysEx Window
from the Window Menu

Quick Tour

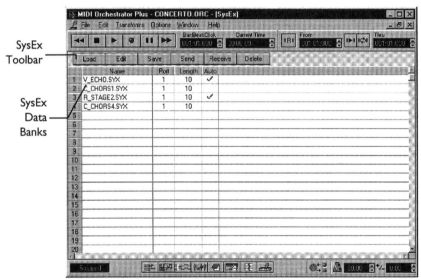

SysEx
Toolbar

SysEx
Data
Banks

The SysEx window

Overview of SysEx

Most modern synthesizers are capable of generating and transmitting a special class of MIDI messages called System Exclusive — or SysEx — messages. Among other things, these messages contain information about patch settings, MIDI configuration parameters and special effects settings like Reverb and Delay.

MIDI Orchestrator Plus allows you to load these messages from your synthesizer, save the data as files and send the messages back to your synthesizer so that they will be available to the synth the next time your song plays.

You can also load existing SysEx files provided by your synth manufacturer, then Save and Send them along with your song.

SysEx messaging functions can be extremely useful for:

- Creating custom patch settings. If the patches are saved in System Exclusive messages along with the song, they will be available to load to the synth the next time the song is played.
- Synths that use effects that can only be programmed with SysEx data. On such synths, you can, for example, send SysEx messages that set specified reverb settings or delay effects.
- Older synthesizers that send real time control information as System Exclusive messages. Some older synthesizers also use SysEx messages to switch banks of programs.

Not all synthesizers use SysEx!

Before you try to work with these functions, be sure to consult your hardware documentation!

The Basic Steps in Using the SysEx Function:

Receive   You load data from your synth into the SysEx window.

Set Auto   If you want the SysEx data to be uploaded — or *Sent* — to your synth when the song is loaded, click the Auto column for the data.

Save   Saves a bank of SysEx data.

Send   If you clicked Auto, this is done automatically when the song loads. To send the SysEx data manually, click this button.

The SysEx Toolbar

Load	Edit	Save	Send	Receive	Delete

Load

 If you have already saved SysEx data files (see below) or if you have SysEx files available from the manufacturer of your synth, you can load up these files and send them to your synth when your song plays.

Clicking the Load button on the Control Bar opens the standard Windows File Open dialog box, enabling to bring one or more data files into the SysEx window. SysEx files use the file extension .SYX.

The data will be loaded into the row you've selected or into the first available row if you haven't selected one. You can select the row by clicking any of its columns or by using the arrow keys to move the selection box into place.

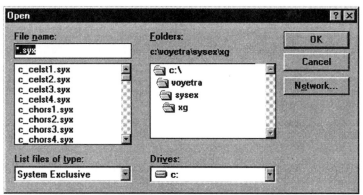

The Windows File Open dialog box
set to load SysEx (.SYX) files
into the SysEx editing window.

To Load SysEx Files from Disk:

1. In the SysEx window, click the row for the bank in which you want the data to appear. If there is already SysEx data in this bank, you will be prompted to append the new data to the existing data or overwrite it.

2. Click the Load button. This opens the standard Windows File Open dialog box.

3. Follow normal Windows procedures to select and load the file.

You can repeat the process for as many files as you want to load into the window, or you can combine data into a single file by loading all the data into the same row.

Edit

 Clicking the Edit button on the SysEx Control Bar opens the Edit SysEx Data dialog box in which you can edit SysEx data directly.

To edit SysEx files you must know Hexadecimal notation and the specific commands for your synthesizer.

If you're not sure of what you're doing, changing SysEx messages can be perilous. It's possible to wipe out pre-existing settings on your synth in the process, so be careful!

Editing specific SysEx messages is beyond the scope of this manual, nevertheless, the following general procedure is included for the advanced user.

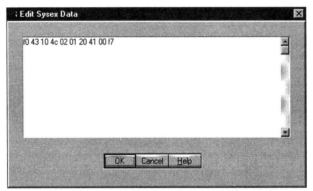

You can edit "raw" SysEx data in this dialog —
BUT BE CAREFUL!
MIDI Orchestrator Plus simply sends
the data to your synth,
it does not verify it!

To Edit SysEx Data:

1. Click the bank you want to edit. If you want to create a new bank of data, click an empty bank.

2. Press the Edit button. A box appears showing the SysEx data in Hex format. You can edit this data directly in the box.

3. When you click OK, the data you entered will be scanned to make sure that the SysEx message begins with F0 and ends with F7. The kind of data displayed between these two numbers will depend on your hardware.

Be EXTREMELY CAREFUL when sending edited data to your synth! If the beginning and ending numbers are correct, MIDI Orchestrator Plus will transmit the messages without verifying the data.

Sending invalid SysEx messages can destroy pre-configured patch settings!

Save any edited SysEx files under a new name and retain the original so that you can restore your synth's settings if necessary.

Save

Clicking the Save button on the SysEx Toolbar opens the Save dialog box where you enter a file name for the data and save it to disk.

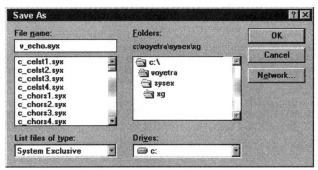

*The Windows Save dialog box
is used to write SysEx files to disk.*

To Save SysEx Files to Disk:

1. In the SysEx window, click the row for the bank you want to save to disk.

2. Click the Save button. This opens the standard Windows File Save dialog box.

3. Follow normal Windows procedures to name, rename or save the file. By default, files are given the extension .SYX.

CAUTION:

If you save your data in .MID rather than .ORC format after sending SysEx data, the following will occur:

*   Bank names and port assignments will be lost.

*   A single bank of data may be split into several smaller banks.

*   If a bank is not set to Auto and does not have an event associated with it, it will not be saved at all!

To avert these problems, we recommend saving your song as an .ORC file.

Changing Numerical Values

To change the values in boxes which accept numerical data, you can use the spin buttons alone or in conjunction with the Shift and Ctrl keys.

For more information about changing numerical values, see the Appendix titled "Changing Numerical Values."

Send

 Clicking the Send button on the SysEx Toolbar opens the Send SysEx Data dialog box showing the progress of the data being sent to your synthesizer.

If you're in the midst of editing a song and you want to change your synth setup while editing, refer to the steps in "Sending Data from the Middle of a Song."

To Send SysEx Data:

1. Click the row in the SysEx window for the bank of SysEx data you want to send.

2. Click the Send button. The Send SysEx Data dialog box appears, showing the progress of the transmission. To send a bank of data automatically, click the Auto column for the bank you want to send. A check mark appears. Now, whenever you load the song, the bank will be sent to your synth.

To Send Data from the Middle of a Song:

1. Make sure that the data you want to send is loaded into one of the banks in the SysEx window.

2. Change to the Event Editor window using the Quick View button at the bottom of the screen.

3. In the Event Editor window, select the track into which you wish to insert the SysEx data.

4. Click Insert or press the Insert key on your computer keyboard to call up the Event Edit dialog box.

5. Press OK to insert the event.

Note that when you send data through the Event Edit dialog box, you are inserting a reference to the SysEx bank, not to the data itself. If you load a different SysEx file into the same bank later in the session, or change the data in the bank, you will lose the original data — only the data currently in the bank will be sent.

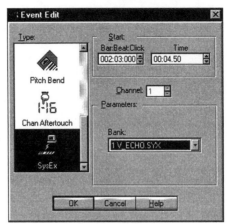

The Event Edit dialog box —
for SysEx

Receiving SysEx Data

 Clicking the Receive button opens the Receive SysEx Data dialog box which allows you to send SysEx data from your synthesizer into the SysEx window. The data can be saved along with the song, and your synth will automatically configure each time you play it.

To Receive a SysEx Data Dump:

1. Click the row in the SysEx window to put the cursor on the bank on which you wish to receive the data.

2. Click the Receive button. The Receive SysEx Data dialog box appears.

3. To receive data automatically, choose your synth in the drop-down Macro list box. Macros for all MIDI devices could not be included, so you may have to use manual receiving if the model of your synth does not appear in the list. Another possibility would be to write your own Macro, documented in the included VSEQINI.WRI file.

If you're receiving manually, choose "You start dump on instrument" from the Macro selection box.

4. You may need to change the Input and Output Port selections in the dialog box depending on the configuration of your MIDI system. If you're using manual receive, you won't need to set an output device. If you do need to make a change, refer to your MIDI hardware manuals for the correct settings.

5. Click OK. If you are using one of the macros, it executes and your MIDI device automatically sends the data to MIDI Orchestrator Plus. In manual mode, the Receiving Data dialog box will appear and you can now begin SysEx transfer from the front panel of your MIDI device. The procedure for doing this will vary widely with different devices, so refer to the appropriate hardware manual for information.

6. As data is received, the count of bytes shown in the Receiving Data dialog box will increase. When the transfer is complete, the number display stops increasing, and your MIDI device will probably give you a visual indication that it has finished transmitting.

7. Click the Done button to accept the received data.

Deleting Data

 Clicking the Delete button on the SysEx Control Bar removes the selected SysEx data file from the window. This does *not* delete the file from your hard drive.

SysEx Window Layout

The SysEx window is built around a row-column structure so that you can easily locate and edit the files and data received.

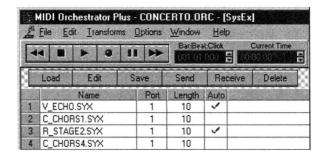

The window is divided into the following columns:

Bank Number

 The column at the far left of the SysEx window numbers SysEx messages in order. You can load a virtually limitless number of messages into a SysEx window — there are 1,000 numbered rows.

Name

Name
V_ECHO.SYX
C_CHORS1.SYX
R_STAGE2.SYX
C_CHORS4.SYX

If your SysEx data already has a file name, it will show up here. If you're receiving data from your synth, rather than loading it from a file, you can name the bank.

Port

Port
1
2
1

This is the port on which your synth sends and receives data. You can change the port assignment for your setup by typing in the number of the port or by right-clicking this column.

Length

Length
10
10
10

This column displays the length of the SysEx file in bytes.

Auto

Clicking the Auto column, toggles the Auto Send feature on and off. A check mark appears in column when you've toggled Auto to the On setting.

With the Auto feature set to On, the SysEx data loaded in the row will be sent to your synth automatically each time the song is loaded.

If you save the song with the Auto feature checked, this becomes a permanent addition to the song file — until you change it by toggling the feature off.

When Auto is set to Off, you send the data manually to the synth by clicking the Send button before playing the song.

Chapter 14

File Menu

Quick Tour

Most of the commands in this menu bring up familiar Windows dialog boxes for opening and saving files. MIDI Orchestrator Plus adds an Audition feature to these standard dialogs so that you can listen to a file before you commit to opening, saving or renaming it.

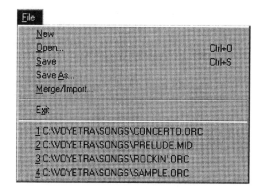

New

Select the New command when you want to create a New file from scratch, clearing all the MIDI Orchestrator Plus windows of data.

Open

This command opens an existing file for playing or editing. If the file you want to open is one of the four most recent you've worked with, you can use the 1,2,3,4... listing at the bottom of the File menu box and avoid navigating through the directories.

Save

This command saves the currently loaded file under its current name.

Save As...

Use Save As to save the current file under a new name or to a different drive or directory. Only .MID, .RMI and .ORC files may be saved.

An .ORC file saves parameters such as: Transpose, Solo, Mute and Controller A and B settings.

If you're saving your file in MIDI format, rather than as an .ORC file, be aware that...

- *If you save a .MID file with tracks Muted, those tracks will be deleted.*

- *If you save your file as a .MID file with tracks Soloed, all of the unsoloed tracks will be deleted.*

File Formats

If you are planning on doing most or all of your work in MIDI Orchestrator Plus, the .ORC format is the one to choose. You can save virtually all your MIDI settings — including SysEx data.

If the choice is between .ORC or one of the MIDI formats, consider the following:

ORC

If you plan to use your file only with your own system or applications that support .ORC files — such as Voyetra's Digital Orchestrator Plus — save your song in Voyetra's proprietary .ORC format. This format preserves all of the file's settings independently, just as you see them on the screen.

MID

For compatibility with most other PC MIDI applications, use the standard .MID format. When you save a file in this format, settings for Tempo, Tempo Offset and Transpose are combined and the resulting new values are saved. **Muted and un-soloed tracks are deleted.**

RMI

Files in this format include a header with identifying information which certain MIDI devices may require. In other respects, .RMI files are identical to standard MIDI files.

SNG

This is the song file format used by the Sequencer Plus series. MIDI Orchestrator Plus can read the .SNG file formats, but it cannot save in that format.

When in doubt, use the .ORC format.

Should you need the file in some other format at a later date, you can always re-open a file and save it again in one of the other formats.

Merge/Import

MIDI Orchestrator Plus lets you merge files to combine a number of different files and file types a single musical composition.

Selecting Merge from the File Menu, brings up the dialog box below.

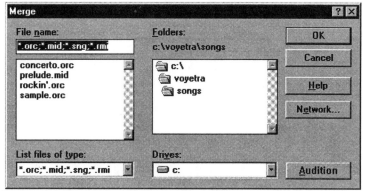

The Merge dialog box lets you navigate to any directory and select a file. When you click OK, MIDI Orchestrator Plus adds the data to the currently open file, beginning with the first available track.

Because you can have only one Conductor Track per file, the Merge command always retains the Conductor track from the currently opened file and discards the Conductor track settings from the new (incoming) file.

For more information on the Conductor track see the "Conductor Editor" and "Event Editor" chapters.

To Merge Files:

1. Open the file containing the conductor track settings you wish to *keep*.

2. From the File menu, select Merge.

3. In the Merge Dialog box, select the .MID, or .ORC file that you wish to insert into the current file, and click OK. A copy of the file you select will merge into the existing file, beginning with the first available track.

If you want to append the new file to the end of the current file, Merge the file, then simply select and drag the new data to the end of the current song.

Exit

Use this command to end a MIDI Orchestrator Plus session.

1,2,3,4...

The four most recently accessed files are listed here, making it simple to re-open the files you have been working with. You can also use this feature to quickly revert to the original saved version of a file.

Chapter 15

Edit Menu

Quick Tour

The commands in the Edit menu are used to edit MIDI tracks. Selected areas and events may be drag-highlighted and then cut or copied into a buffer similar to the Windows Clipboard. This buffer, however, is internal to MIDI Orchestrator Plus and cannot be used to exchange data with other Windows programs. Only the Notepad can be used to cut, copy or paste information between MIDI Orchestrator Plus and other Windows applications.

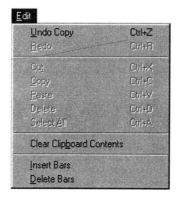

Selecting Data

Before you can edit data, you have to select it. You can do this in a number of ways — by clicking, clicking-and-dragging or using the keyboard.

Click

In windows that use the row and column format, simply click a row or column to select it. The row or track need not have data in it. In certain instances, such as recording to a new track or loading SysEx data, the data is sent to the selected row. Clicking the Track Number in the Bar Pane of the Track/View window selects the entire track.

Click-and-Drag

You select an area of data by clicking the mouse, holding down the left mouse button, and dragging — horizontally, vertically or diagonally — across the material you want to select. The area between the beginning and the ending points of the drag is highlighted to indicate the selection.

From the Computer Keyboard

In several windows, you can use the arrow keys to move the cursor or highlight data. By holding down the Shift key while moving the cursor you can also select data.

Edit Menu Commands

The follow are the commands, and their Keyboard Shortcut Keys, available in the Edit Menu:

Undo

The Undo command lets you reverse the effect of up to 12 of the most recent editing commands. The available command depends on the last command that was executed. If that command was Undo, then Redo becomes available. This lets you toggle between and audition the edited and unedited versions of your file, as well as Undo up to 12 levels of edits.

For example, if you perform a drag edit, delete a note, and then decide you didn't want to do either, you can Undo both actions. Just select Undo Delete Note from the Edit menu, then select Undo Drag Edit from the Edit menu and you're back where you started.

You can change the number of available Undo levels from the default of 12 by editing the ORCHPLUS.INI file with a text editor. For more information, read the VSEQINI.WRI file. Increasing the number of Undo levels demands additional memory.

Keyboard Shortcut Key: Ctrl+Z

Redo

This command lets you Redo an Undo and, like the Undo command, operates up to 12 levels deep. The Redo you see will be based on the edits and Undos that you've executed. You perform multiple Redos in the same way as you do the Undos: just keep selecting the available Redo from the Edit menu. For more information, see Undo.

Keyboard Shortcut Key: Ctrl+R

Cut

This command lets you remove a selected area or event and place it into the Clipboard where it can be pasted to another location. The Cut command does not leave a copy of the data behind.

Keyboard Shortcut Key: Ctrl+X

Copy

The Copy command sends a copy of any selected data to the MIDI Orchestrator Plus Clipboard. Unlike Cut, the Copy command makes a duplicate of selected data, leaving the original data behind unaltered.

The data can then be pasted into another location in the window, into another MIDI Orchestrator Plus window or into another instance of a window.

Keyboard Shortcut Key: Ctrl+C

Paste

This command lets you paste whatever is in the Clipboard to a new location defined by the current cursor position or a highlighted area.

You can paste data into another location in the same MIDI Orchestrator Plus window and you can cut-and-paste between windows or between separate instances of the same window. For example, you can select a note in Piano Roll and paste it into the Event Editor window. If you're pasting data in the Event List, a pop up dialog box will ask you for the location of the desired paste.

You can paste the same segment of data into many locations. MIDI Orchestrator Plus places a reference to the data rather than the data itself into the file when you cut-and-paste or copy-and-paste.

If you don't want the data to merge with existing material at the
location of the paste, select an area of a MIDI file before using the paste
command. When you Paste, the contents of the Clipboard will replace
any existing data, beginning at the starting point of your selection. If
you didn't select a range, the data will merge, beginning at the point
where you clicked the mouse.

Keyboard Shortcut Key: Ctrl+V

Delete

Use this command to remove the selected area or event. This differs
from the Copy command in that it does not place any information into
the Clipboard. This is useful for removing data that you no longer need
and it does not use any extra memory by placing the data into the
Clipboard.

Keyboard Shortcut Key: Ctrl+D

Select All

When you want to select all of the tracks in a song, this is the
command to use. You will find that Select All is faster than highlighting
the entire song!

Keyboard Shortcut Key: Ctrl+A

Clear Clipboard Contents

When you cut or copy a selected area or event and place it on the Clipboard, it remains there indefinitely — until you cut or copy something else to the Clipboard. However, once you have pasted the contents of the Clipboard to a new location and no longer require the data, clearing the contents of the Clipboard can help speed up processing.

The Clear Clipboard Contents command serves two functions — it clears the contents of the Clipboard and any Undo information being stored. Remember, MIDI Orchestrator Plus holds up to 12 levels of Undo (unless you have changed this default setting), so that you can reverse the effect of up to 12 of the most recent editing commands.

Clicking Clear Clipboard Contents displays a warning box to verify that you do indeed want to proceed with this action. Click OK if you are certain that you will not require the Clipboard Contents and the Undo information being retained.

The Clear Clipboard Contents command clears BOTH the Contents of the Clipboard and the Undo information being stored.

BE CAREFUL — this action CANNOT be undone!

Once the contents of the Clipboard and Undo information have been cleared, they are gone forever!

Insert Bars

This command opens the Insert Bars dialog box, letting you insert blank bars into a specified location.

Before Bars

Use this field to set the starting position of the Bars you want to insert. When you open the Insert Bars dialog box, the current cursor position is shown as the Before Bars setting.

Number of Bars

Enter the number of bars you want to insert.

Track

Insert bars in any one track or all of the tracks at once.

Time Signature

You can set the Numerator, Denominator and Number of Beats per bar for the bars you are inserting. For more information, see the "Conductor Editor" and "Piano Roll" chapters.

Delete Bars

Choosing this command opens the Delete Bars dialog box. This dialog lets you delete bars, blank or otherwise, shifting the data to the left to fill in the space of the deleted bars.

If you want to delete data and replace it with an interval of silence, you can use Delete Bars to remove the data and then add blank bars using the Insert Bars command — or you can cut the data using the Edit menu's Cut command.

Beginning Bar

Use the cursor to mark the delete start point, or enter a value.

Number of Bars

Enter a value or — if you've highlighted a range — it appears as the Number of Bars setting when you open the dialog.

Track

Any number of tracks — or All tracks — may be selected and deleted.

Chapter 16

Transforms Menu

Transforms

Set Velocity...
Offset Velocity...
Quantize Note Duration...
Quantize Note...

MIDI Orchestrator Plus' transforms enable you to select and change a portion of your song file in a single operation. Transforms work on a selected portion of a file so, if you select across tracks, the transform will be applied to all the data throughout the selected ranges.

In general, you use a transform when you want to make a permanent change to your file; however, MIDI Orchestrator Plus' Undo feature allows you to reverse any changes you've made and try other settings.

By alternating between Undo and Redo you can compare the sound with and without the transform.

Applying a Transform

The transforms and their parameter settings are described in detail in this chapter. The procedure for using the transforms is just about the same for all of the transforms and is described in the steps below:

To Apply a Transform:

1. From any window that is convenient, select the MIDI notes or MIDI measures you wish to change.
2. From the Transforms menu, select the desired transform.
3. When a dialog box appears, enter or adjust the parameters as needed. (The effects of the various Transform options are explained in this chapter.)
4. Click OK.
5. Listen to the file to check the results. If necessary, use the Undo command to restore the file, run the transform again and adjust the settings.

Velocity Transforms

This category of Transforms affect a note's Velocity. Velocity is a measure of how a key was struck when the note was played. Values can range from 1 (a very gentle touch) to the maximum of 127 (a very hard hit). At playback, Velocity usually controls the loudness, or dynamics, of your piece. Depending on your synthesizer, it may also affect brightness or other musical qualities.

By changing Velocity values, you can change the dynamics of individual notes or groups of notes. Transforming dynamics can dramatically change the mood of your music.

Note that some synthesizers cannot transmit velocity information and simply assign the same value to every note. A particular synthesizer may or may not respond to velocity messages during playback. Refer to your synthesizer's documentation to find out about velocity messages.

If the Velocity is zero, the note won't play at all. For this reason, all of the transforms limit the resulting Velocities to a range from 1 to 127. At very low velocities, notes may be inaudible.

Set Velocity

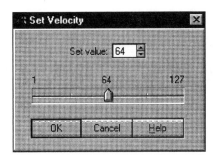

This command opens the Set Velocity dialog box.

Set Velocity enables you to set the Velocity for all selected notes to the same value. You can use the slider or the Set value box to enter the desired value, from 1 to 127.

Offset Velocity

This command opens the Offset Velocity dialog box.

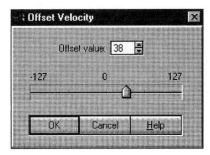

Offset Velocity lets you increase or decrease the existing Velocity of notes in a selected range by the Offset value that you choose. This preserves the dynamics with which the music was originally played, while adjusting the overall velocities.

Quantize Note Duration

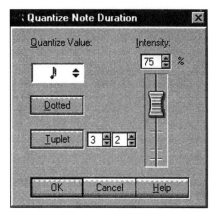

This command opens the Quantize Note Duration dialog box.

Quantize Note Duration sets the duration of notes to the nearest even multiple of a selected value. If, for example, you choose a quarter note as the value, each note will be converted to a quarter note, half note, a whole note, etc. — whatever value is nearest to its original duration.

The Quantization Value can be from a 64th note to a quarter note in length. You can also select dotted notes or tuplets.

You can control the Intensity of the quantization effect. For example, if you set the intensity to 75%, each note's duration will move only three-quarters of the way to its target.

Quantize Note...

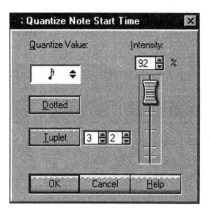

This command opens **the Quantize Note Start Time dialog.**

Quantize Note Start Time lets you adjust the start times of the selected notes so they begin only at certain points in the measure. For example, if you played a series of notes off the beat, you can quantize their start times, so they begin precisely on the beat.

In Quantize Note Start Time, a variety of options permit detailed control over which notes are affected and the quality of the results:

Quantize Value This is a timing value, expressed as a musical note from a 64th note to a quarter note in length. It may help to imagine a grid superimposed on the measure. Notes are moved toward lines of the grid. The quantize value establishes the value between grid lines.

If, for example, you select an eighth note as the value, the beginning of each selected note will move to the nearest eighth note division within the measure.

Dotted This control adjusts the start times of notes to the nearest dotted note value. This option is most suitable for time signatures with numerators that are divisible by three, such as 3/4 or 6/8. When measures cannot be divided evenly into dotted note intervals, the grid is re-aligned at the beginning of each measure.

Tuplet When selected, this control divides the measure into tuplet intervals. The Tuplets feature lets you specify a non-standard duration for a note, such as a triplet or a quintuplet. For example, if you wanted to insert a quarter note triplet, you would select a quarter note in the box above the tuplet control and set the Tuplets ratio to 3:2. This sets the grid to three notes in the space normally taken by two quarter notes.

Intensity Intensity controls the degree of quantization. This guards against making your music overly precise and mechanical. If you set the intensity to 75%, each note will move only three-quarters of the way to the nearest grid point.

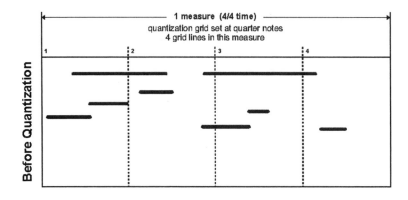

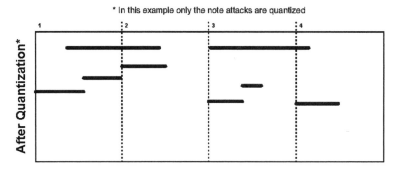

* In this example only the note attacks are quantized

These charts shows how quantization settings affect notes. Notice that in the second chart — After Quantization — the notes line up neatly on the grid. This gives the piece a much tighter sound and feel.

You can disrupt playback by moving note events without moving corresponding non-note events such as patch or controller changes.

In general, when moving note events, move the non-note events following them as well.

Chapter 17

Options Menu

The Options menu could also be called the "configuration" or "setup" menu.

This menu lets you customize MIDI Orchestrator Plus according to the hardware you have installed and your personal preferences.

MIDI Thru

When checked, MIDI Thru is turned on, allowing MIDI data to be echoed to the MIDI Out port. If you are using a keyboard that plays through your sound card, you'll hear the sound through your computer's speakers or headphones only when MIDI Thru is set to On. On is the default setting for this option. If MIDI Thru is On, whatever channels you are transmitting in will be echoed to the same channel on all output ports.

Save Settings on Exit

When this option is checked, MIDI Orchestrator Plus saves the current screen and configuration settings when you close the program and it restores them when you open the program.

Metronome Settings

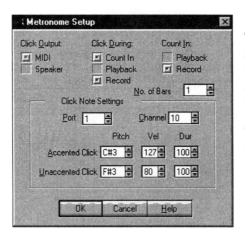

This command opens the Metronome Setup dialog box in which you can set the Metronome's various options.

You can set the Metronome's click to play through the PC speaker or as a percussive note sounded on a MIDI device like a drum machine.

You also can control whether the metronome is heard on playback, during recording, or both.

Click Output

This setting determines whether a MIDI device, the PC speaker or both will be used to sound the Metronome's click.

Click During

These options let you choose if the Metronome will sound during Count In, Recording or Playback. You can select any combination, none or all three.

Count In

This setting lets you choose whether or not you will hear the Metronome count in during playback and record.

No. of Bars

You can set this value to the number of measures you want for the Count In.

The beats per measure and the accent click are determined by the time signature chosen in the Event list.

Port

 This box lets you select the output port for the metronome MIDI click.

The default is port 1, the port to which your sound card is most likely to be connected.

Channel

 This box lets you select the output channel for the MIDI metronome note.

The default is channel 10, the General MIDI percussion channel. If you are using a sound card with Base Level MIDI, select channel 16.

Accented Click

In this section of the dialog box, you can set the Pitch, Velocity, and Duration of the accented (louder) click, which corresponds to the downbeat of each measure.

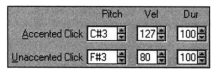

Accented and Unaccented Click

Unaccented Click

In this section of the dialog box you can set the Pitch, Velocity, and Duration of the unaccented (quieter) click, which corresponds to the other beats in each measure.

You'll probably want to use the same percussion "note" for both accented and unaccented metronome clicks. A short percussive sound is usually better than a longer sound or melodic instrument. Default is the Side Stick (C#3), but the Hi-Hat sound (F#3) also works well. See the Appendix for a complete listing of MIDI percussion sounds.

MIDI Port Setup

MIDI data is sent and received among MIDI devices through connections called MIDI ports. In order for a MIDI port to work, the device driver for the sound card or MIDI interface must be installed according to the manufacturer's directions.

The MIDI Port Setup command opens the MIDI Port Setup dialog box where you can select any one of the installed drivers for each input and output port.

If you encounter difficulties with any of the MIDI Port Options, run MediaCheck,™ Voyetra's multimedia diagnostic utility. You'll find the MediaCheck icon in your MIDI Orchestrator Plus program group. For more information on MediaCheck, refer to the Appendix of this manual.

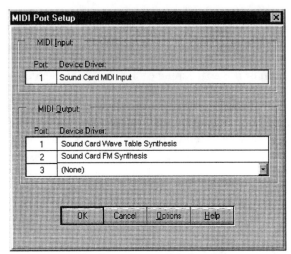

MIDI Port Setup Dialog Box

The Options button in the MIDI Port Setup dialog box opens a nested dialog — the MIDI Options dialog box.

Use the MIDI Options dialog box to configure MIDI Orchestrator Plus for parallel port interfaces or to select a clock speed.

The three MIDI Options are:

- Close Drivers While Printing
- Keep MIDI Drivers Open While Inactive
- Send Reset Controllers on Stop

Close Drivers While Printing

This setting allows you to print with MIDI interfaces that connect to the computer's parallel port (such as Voyetra's VP-11). Normally, these interfaces disable the parallel port when MIDI Orchestrator Plus is running, making it impossible to print musical notation.

To Enable Printing with Parallel Port MIDI Interfaces:

1. From the Options menu, select MIDI Port Setup.
2. In the MIDI Port Setup dialog box, click the Options button.
3. Select Close Drivers While Printing, then Click OK.

Keep MIDI Drivers Open While Inactive

Whenever you're working in MIDI Orchestrator Plus, your MIDI drivers are open, allowing you to play and record songs. However, you might want to open another program while MIDI Orchestrator Plus is running, taking advantage of Windows' ability to multitask.

The Keep MIDI Drivers Open While Inactive setting determines how your MIDI configuration changes when you switch from MIDI Orchestrator Plus to a different Windows program.

If you deselect this option, you'll find that your external MIDI keyboard doesn't make sound when another program is active. MIDI Orchestrator Plus has closed down the MIDI drivers, including those for your MIDI In and MIDI Thru.

With this Option selected, the MIDI functions are not available to other MIDI programs that may be running. This will cause conflicts and system instability if different MIDI programs try to access the drivers at the same time.

Send Reset Controllers on Stop

If your MIDI scores involve lots of controller changes events, you will probably want to select this option. If, for example, you have the Volume and Pan controllers changing to simulate the motion of a musician moving around a stage and you stop the song, auto-rewind, then play it back, Volume and Pan will be set to the values at the stop playback position.

By enabling Send Reset Controllers on Stop, you can prevent this type of subtle error. MIDI Orchestrator Plus will reset all the controllers so that every song starts out clean, with no controller remnants from a previous song or playback session.

Clock Rate

Clock rate sets the number of clicks per quarter note. This is the "click" shown in MIDI Orchestrator Plus' Bar:Beat:Click controls.

If MIDI Orchestrator Plus appears to start playing but halts immediately, before any note is played, you may need to adjust the Clock Rate. Here's how:

To Set the Clock Rate:

1. From the Options menu, select MIDI Port Setup.
2. In the MIDI Port Setup dialog box, click the Options button.
3. From the Clock Rate list, select Low, then click OK.
4. Use the fastest clock speed that works for your system.

Patch Map Setup

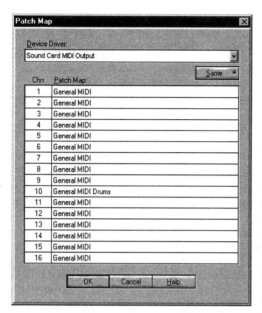

This command opens the Patch Map Setup dialog box which lets you choose one of the installed patch maps customized for popular MIDI modules and synthesizers.

This dialog box displays a drop-down list box where you can choose any of the installed drivers. When you do, the Channel (Chn) and Patch Map settings show which Patch Map is being used on which channel for the selected driver.

To Select a Patch Map:

1. From the Patch Map Setup dialog box, click the arrow on the right of the Device Driver drop-down box. A list displaying the available MIDI Output drivers appears.

2. Scroll through the list until you find the MIDI Output driver you want to set a patch map for. Click the name of the driver.

3. Double-click in the drop-down box of the track whose Patch Map you want to change. Click the name of the Patch Map.

4. If you want to assign Patch Maps individually for different channels, repeat the procedure above for each channel.

5. If you want to set all 16 channels to use the same Patch Map, activate the Same button (the green light will come on), then select a Patch Map for any channel.

6. Click OK.

After you have selected the desired Patch Maps, click with the right mouse button on the Patch column in the Track/View window. This brings up a dialog box from which you can select any of the available patch names or numbers.

 The next time you go to change a Patch Map, you may not immediately see the driver you last selected in the Device Driver list. This is because the Device Drivers are not listed in the same order as they appear in the MIDI Port Setup. Scroll down to locate the Device Driver you want, you will notice that it retains the changes you previously made.

Controllers

This option lets you assign two MIDI Controllers of your choice to the knobs in the Mixer window and to the corresponding columns in the Track window. Clicking this item displays a dialog box from which you can choose the Controllers you prefer.

The available Controllers are listed in the Appendix at the back of this book. Check the documentation for your MIDI device to see if it will respond to the Controller you wish to use.

The default Controllers are 091 (Reverb) and 093 (Chorus).

Chapter 18

Window Menu

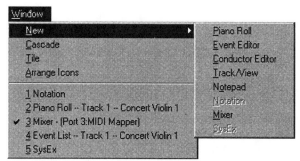

Window menu with its flyout menu

The Window menu can be used to open individual editing windows and arrange the windows in the Workspace. Use the Window menu to open additional instances of editing windows that support multiple views.

New

Use the New command to open additional copies of the editing windows. You can open multiple instances of the Piano Roll, Event Editor, and Mixer windows. However, you can open only a single instance of the Notation Window, Conductor Editor, Track/View, Notepad, and SysEx windows. In general, it's easier to use the Quick View buttons on the Main window's Status Bar to open an editing window if you only require a single instance of the window.

Cascade

The Cascade command arranges all of the open editing windows — except those reduced to icon size — in the familiar overlapping fashion.

Tile

The Tile command arranges all of the open editing windows — except those reduced to icon size — without overlapping them.

Arrange Icons

Arrange icons arranges any editing window icons starting at the bottom left of the Main window Workspace.

1, 2, 3, 4...

This list shows all current editing windows, including any that are minimized. A check mark shows which are active. To bring any window to the foreground, you can click its name in the list or type its number from the keyboard.

Chapter 19

Help Menu

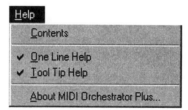

MIDI Orchestrator Plus offers four ways of accessing Help::

- An extensive on-line help system is available when you select Help from the menu. You can also press the F1 key to open the context-sensitive Help feature which will display information about the currently selected command or control.
- One Line Help messages display in the Main window's Title Bar when the cursor remains on a control for a second or two.
- Most dialog boxes have Help buttons which take you directly to the Help screen for that topic.
- Tool Tips identify the name of the control when the mouse remains over a control for a few seconds. Tool Tips also appear, after a brief delay, over column headings in the Track/View window.

Contents

Opens the Help file at the Table of Contents page.

One Line Help

This menu option toggles One Line Help On and Off. (On is the default setting for this feature; a check mark indicates that One Line Help is active.) One Line Help provides a single-line definition of screen areas and controls as you pass your mouse pointer over them. The One Line Help text is displayed in the Title Bar at the top of the screen.

Tool Tips

When you move your mouse pointer over a control or a column heading, a small box appears which identifies the control or heading. Like One Line Help, this feature can be toggled On and Off by selecting it in the menu. A check mark indicates that this feature is active.

About MIDI Orchestrator

Clicking this menu item displays the version and release date, as well as the Product ID number of the copy of MIDI Orchestrator Plus you are working with.

Chapter 20

MediaCheck

MediaCheck™ provides an easy way to test and troubleshoot the digital audio and MIDI features of your computer. A series of displays takes you through the testing process step-by-step. If, for some reason, one of the multimedia devices on your computer is not working properly, MediaCheck provides troubleshooting tips to help you get your system up-and-running again.

MediaCheck also provides setup tips for attaching an external MIDI keyboard to your computer — and a video to show you how to make these connections. Once the MIDI cable is installed, you can use MediaCheck's MIDI Input and MIDI Output tests to confirm that your system is operating properly.

When troubleshooting a multimedia computer, it is often necessary to view the installed sound card drivers if changes need to be made to the drivers' configuration. Locating these drivers can be quite difficult. The Advanced button in MediaCheck calls up SoundCheck,™ an advanced multimedia troubleshooting utility, which displays a detailed listing of all of your computer's sound card drivers. From here you can access the drivers' configuration dialog box and view status information. This tells you whether the driver is working properly — or not. SoundCheck also provides access to the Windows MIDI and Sound Mapper applications.

MediaCheck Main Screen

Here's an overview of the main screen in MediaCheck. Note that clicking the Advanced button calls up SoundCheck, which takes a more detailed look at your system.

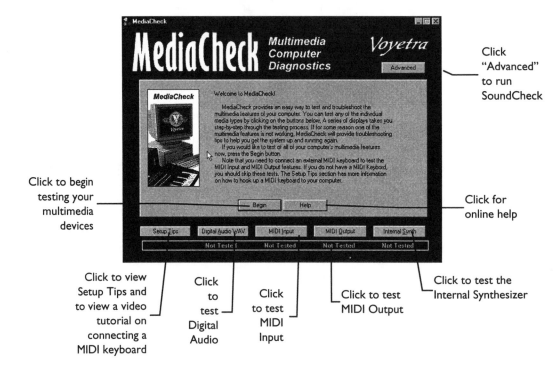

Click "Advanced" to run SoundCheck

Click to begin testing your multimedia devices

Click for online help

Click to view Setup Tips and to view a video tutorial on connecting a MIDI keyboard

Click to test Digital Audio

Click to test MIDI Input

Click to test MIDI Output

Click to test the Internal Synthesizer

Using MediaCheck

With MediaCheck, you can run a complete test of your multimedia devices or individually test the specific multimedia functions you are having trouble with. For example, you may want to perform a complete test before your run a multimedia application or you may only want to run the MIDI Input Test if you just hooked up an external MIDI keyboard to your PC and want to make certain it is working properly.

Running the Complete Test

The complete test checks Digital Audio, MIDI Input, MIDI Output, and Internal Synth.

To run the complete test:

1. Click the Begin button on the main screen. MediaCheck automatically takes you step-by-step through the various tests.
2. In each test, you are prompted with questions to help determine that your system is working correctly. Click the appropriate answer for each question.

Running a Specific Test

If you only need to test a specific function — for example, Digital Audio or MIDI Input or Output — there's no need to run a complete test.

To Run an Individual Test:

1. Click the button for the test you would like to perform. These buttons are located along the bottom of the MediaCheck screen.
2. Once a test has started, you are prompted with questions to help determine that your system is working correctly. Click the appropriate answer for each question.

Test Results

As the test advances, MediaCheck provides feedback. This information appears beneath the test button.

Test Passed   Indicates your system is working correctly.

Test Failed   Indicates your system is not working correctly.

Not Tested   Indicates that test has not been run yet.

Setup Tips

The Setup Tips section includes a video which demonstrates how to connect the MIDI cable to your PC and MIDI keyboard.

To View Setup Tips:

- Click the Setup Tips button located at the bottom of the screen.

 For additional information on connecting your MIDI keyboard to your PC, refer to "Making the Connections" in the "Up and Running" chapter.

Digital Audio WAV Test

The Digital Audio WAV Test provides a quick check of the digital audio playback capabilities of your multimedia system.

To Run the Digital Audio WAV Test:

1. Click the Digital Audio WAV Test button at the bottom of the screen. This will play a digital audio file.
2. When asked if you can hear it, click either Yes or No.
3. Your answer determines the next course of action.
    - If you choose Yes, MediaCheck assumes that your system is functioning properly.
    - If you choose No, MediaCheck suggests several trouble-shooting tips. Try these tips. If one of these works, you should hear the WAV file. If none works, click the Advanced button for more information about your system's WAV drivers.

MIDI Input Test

The MIDI Input Test provides an easy way to check that MIDI data is being received from an external source — such as a MIDI keyboard.

To Run the MIDI Input Test:

1. Be sure your MIDI keyboard is connected to your computer.
2. Click the MIDI Input Test button at the bottom of the screen.
3. Click the correct answer for the questions asked.
   - When the keyboard is played, one of the 16 lights should illuminate. For example, if the keyboard is transmitting on MIDI Channel 1, the Channel 1 light illuminates.
   - Each of the 16 lights represents a MIDI input channel. This helps you determine which channel your MIDI keyboard is transmitting on.
   - If none of the MIDI input lights are blinking, click the No button and follow the troubleshooting tips.

MIDI Output Test

The MIDI Output Test provides an easy way to check that MIDI data is being transmitted successfully from your computer to an external source — such as a MIDI synth.

To Run the MIDI Output Test:

1. Be sure your MIDI keyboard is connected to your computer.
2. Click the MIDI Output Test button at the bottom of the screen.
3. When asked if you can hear the MIDI file, click Yes or No.
   - If the synth is turned on and connected properly you should hear music coming from the synth.
   - If you cannot hear music playing from the synth, it is not connected properly. Click the No button and follow the troubleshooting tips.

MIDI Drum Sounds

MIDI files transmit their information on different channels, and each channel is usually assigned a different musical instrument sound. Typically drum sounds are fixed to either channel 10 or channel 16. This can sometimes cause a problem.

For example, a game may play a MIDI file with its drum information programmed on channel 16, but the internal synthesizer is set to play its drum sounds on channel 10. This would cause the music to sound strange. Usually the multimedia application provides a way to fix this.

MediaCheck can help by confirming which channel your computer's internal synthesizer has drums mapped to.

Internal MIDI Synthesizer Test

Most multimedia computers have a MIDI synthesizer built in. This enables games and other multimedia applications to play music. Unlike digital audio, MIDI does not put a lot of strain on the system's processor. Also, MIDI files are much smaller than digital audio files.

To Run the Internal MIDI Synthesizer Test:

1. Click the Internal MIDI Synthesizer Test button. A MIDI file plays a drum part on channel 10.
    *   If you hear drums, click Yes and move on to the next test.
    *   If you hear a sound like a "piano playing a strange melody," click No.
2. When you click No, MediaCheck plays a MIDI drum part on channel 16. If you don't hear anything at this point, there may be a problem with the internal synthesizer in your system or its drivers.
3. Follow the on-screen instructions for information on how to resolve this type of problem.

Advanced Button

The Advanced button in MediaCheck launches SoundCheck, which takes a more detailed look at your multimedia hardware and software. SoundCheck displays all of the sound card drivers currently installed on your system along with the status of each. This information helps determine if there is a problem — such as an address or interrupt conflict — with the hardware or software.

To Launch SoundCheck:

- Click the Advanced button at the upper right of the screen.

 Do NOT wear headphones when using SoundCheck! Running the tests in SoundCheck can cause sudden volume increases.

SoundCheck Screen

Displays information about the Wave Drivers

Displays information about the MIDI Drivers

Displays information about the CD-ROM Drivers

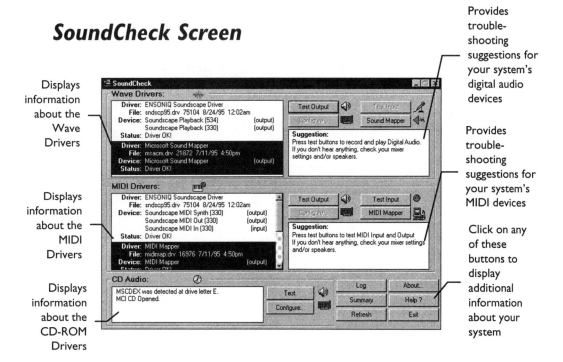

Provides trouble-shooting suggestions for your system's digital audio devices

Provides trouble-shooting suggestions for your system's MIDI devices

Click on any of these buttons to display additional information about your system

Testing Digital Audio

MIDI Orchestrator Plus does NOT use digital audio. Registered owners of MIDI Orchestrator Plus can upgrade to Voyetra's Digital Orchestrator Plus, which does. The following sections describe digital audio and CD audio for the benefit of running our MediaCheck™ and SoundCheck™ diagnostic programs.

To Test Digital Audio Output:

1. Click the Test Output button, in the Wave Drivers section, to play a pre-recorded test file.
2. A dialog box asks whether the file is playing. If there is no sound, check the most likely sources of problems:
   - Speakers are connected incorrectly.
   - Low sound card volume setting.
   - Speakers or other amplified source is not turned on or the volume setting is too low.

To Test Digital Audio Input:

If you are not able to record sound, the problem could simply be bad connections or your drivers may be set up incorrectly. Follow these steps to isolate the problem:

1. Connect a microphone or other device — such as a tape deck — to the appropriate input on your sound card.
2. Use the Mixer utility that came with your Sound Card to select the input device and set the volume level.
3. Click the Test Input button in the Wave Drivers section. The Wave Input Test dialog box opens.
4. Click the Record button.
5. Speak into the microphone for a few seconds — or play a few seconds of the tape.
6. Click the Stop button in the dialog box to stop recording.
7. Click the Play button to hear the results. If you don't hear anything, continue on to Configuring Digital Audio.

Configuring Digital Audio

Before you make any changes to your Wave Driver's configuration, consult your sound card manual.

To Configure Digital Audio:

*   Click the Configure button in the Wave Drivers section. SoundCheck displays a dialog box enabling you to change the configuration of the currently-selected driver.

You should change the driver configuration ONLY if you have a problem. Most often, you need to restart Windows for any changes to take effect. If you do not restart Windows, click the Refresh button so that SoundCheck can recognize the new configuration.

Testing MIDI Output

To Test MIDI Output:

*   Click the Test Output button in the MIDI Drivers section. The MIDI Output Test dialog box opens. From here you can play a Base Level, Extended Level or Dual Arrangement MIDI test file. This helps determine which MIDI setup is best for your system.

Unless you have selected it for testing, SoundCheck bypasses the MIDI Mapper and sends MIDI data directly to the device driver. This helps you distinguish between incorrect MIDI Mapper settings and problems with the driver software.

Testing MIDI Input

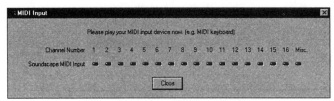

The MIDI Input Dialog Box

To Test MIDI Input:

- Click the Test Input button in the MIDI Drivers section. This opens the MIDI Test Input dialog box.

MIDI input testing allows you to quickly determine:

- If MIDI data sent from a MIDI device is reaching your computer.
- On which channel MIDI data is being received.

A row of 17 LEDs appears in the MIDI Input dialog box. The first 16 correspond to the 16 MIDI channels; the 17th LED, the one at the far right labeled "Misc," is for non-note MIDI messages that are not channel-specific. As you play a synthesizer or other MIDI device, one or more of the LEDs flash to indicate when MIDI data is being received and on which channel.

MIDI

To Configure MIDI:

- Click the MIDI Mapper button to open the Windows MIDI configuration utility.

In Windows 3.1:

- It opens the MIDI Mapper.

In Windows 95:

- It opens the MIDI Properties dialog box.

Use either utility to choose an appropriate setup for your MIDI output device, edit an existing setup or create new ones. As a general guide:

- Base Level synths, typically the earlier FM synthesis sound cards, only use channels 11 through 16, with drums on channel 16.
- Extended Level synths, typically better FM synthesis sound cards, use channels 1 through 10, with drums on channel 10.
- General MIDI synths, typically wavetable synthesis sound cards or external high-end keyboard systems, use all 16 MIDI channels, with drums on channel 10.

Testing CD Audio

A message in the status box in the CD Audio section tells you whether or not MSCDEX was detected. If it is detected, a second message informs you of the status of the Windows MCI CD audio driver. If SoundCheck tells you that MSCDEX was not detected, refer your CD-ROM drive's manual for the proper installation of MSCDEX.

To Test CD Audio:

1. Place a disc with audio tracks in the CD-ROM drive. Use a commercial CD recording — the kind you buy in a record store.
2. Check your mixer settings. Be sure that the CD-ROM drive is selected and that the volume is turned up enough.
3. Click the Test button to play a CD Audio track.

Summary Button

The Summary screen displays an overview of your system's audio capabilities. You can also run a speed diagnostic of your system from this screen.

Not all sound cards actually play at precisely the same sample rate. SoundCheck can measure how accurate the playback of your sound card is.

At the bottom of this screen is the Wave Sync button. This runs a diagnostic to test the actual sample rates of your sound card.

To Run a Speed Diagnostic of Your System:

1. Click the Summary button to open the Audio Capabilities & Related Data screen.
2. Click the Run button to test your system's speed.

Log Button

The Log button opens Notepad and creates a log file containing extensive configuration information.

This file contains data generated during testing that can be useful to you and to tech support people.

Wave Sync

Wave Sync tests your hardware's ability to accurately synchronize digital audio and MIDI.

 It is only necessary to use Wave Sync if you are working with applications that have this option — such as Voyetra's Digital Orchestrator Plus.™

To Test Wave Sync:

1. In SoundCheck, click Summary to display the Audio Capabilities & Related Data dialog box. Then click WaveSync.
2. Choose the Wave Out Device. (This is how sound will be played out of your sound card. Usually you will see the name of the sound card displayed in this box.)
3. Select the Sample Rate to test.
4. Click the Start button.
5. When you are done, also check the Wave In Device by selecting "None" for Wave Out and selecting the sound card for Wave In.

You will notice numbers calculating. Note that this may take a LONG time.

Here's an explanation of the terms used in the Wave Sync test:

Elapsed Time Is a measure of how much time has passed, in milliseconds, since you clicked the Start button.

Actual Sample Rate Is the true sample rate of the sound card. As time passes, the accuracy of this number increases. You will be able to see the Actual Sample Rate number begin to stabilize as time goes on.

Deviation Is the running margin of error that your sound card's drivers may produce.

What the Deviation numbers mean:

Between 0 and 10 Excellent for syncing digital audio and MIDI.

Between 11 and 50 Good for syncing digital audio and MIDI.

Between 50 and 500 Fair (it may be a bit unstable) for syncing digital audio and MIDI.

Over 500 Syncing digital audio and MIDI will not work.

Be aware that many sound cards have a very low Wave Out deviation and a high Wave In deviation.

The timing of digital audio playback is handled solely by your sound card driver. If you have a multimedia program that synchronizes digital audio with another function — such as MIDI to WAV — it must ask the sound card exactly where into the playback of the WAV file it is at any moment. This information is gathered by the application communicating with your sound card's WAV driver. This information is then used to calculate at what point the WAV file should sound. If there is a large discrepancy in this number — where the sound is and where the sound card driver thinks it is — the application will not play the sound at the correct moment. This can result in an out-of-sync playback.

Appendix A

Overview of MIDI

MIDI, an acronym for Musical Instrument Digital Interface, is a system for encoding, sending and receiving the electronic messages which control MIDI devices. Anything that generates or responds to MIDI messages is a MIDI device. Common MIDI devices are electronic musical synthesizers (synths), keyboards, and drum machines. MIDI commands can also control more specialized devices, such as theatrical lighting systems. A sound card installed in a computer can also be programmed to respond to MIDI commands.

MIDI is not a product or a tangible object; it is a specification — a widely accepted system of rules — introduced in the early 1980s by the MIDI Manufacturers Association. These rules specify how MIDI data should be encoded and sent among MIDI devices. They also govern hardware issues such as the design of the cables and connectors used by MIDI devices.

A series of MIDI commands can be organized in a deliberate way to instruct a MIDI synthesizer to play a musical passage. This series of commands is called a *sequence* and a hardware device or computer software program that creates and edits sequences is called a *sequencer*. With sequencer software, your computer can record, edit, or play MIDI sequences and save them as files on a disk. The collection of commands in a file — the sequence — then instructs a synthesizer to play the music.

A single MIDI sequence can control a number of MIDI devices — virtually an entire synthesized orchestra. This requires certain procedures to keep things organized. For example, to ensure that each command reaches the correct device, each MIDI command includes an instruction that assigns it to a MIDI port. If a command is assigned to port 1, only the MIDI device attached to port 1 receives the command.

Each command routed to a given port is also assigned one of 16 MIDI channels. Like a television, a MIDI device receives incoming signals on all channels, and can be set to respond only to selected channels. A synthesizer differs from a TV, however, in that it can "tune in" more than one channel at a time.

Each channel is assigned a patch — an instruction that tells the synthesizer to generate a particular type of instrumental sound for that channel. So, for example, if you have assigned an oboe patch to port 2, channel 4, any note directed to port 2, channel 4 will sound like an oboe — until you change the patch assignment.

MIDI commands can trigger two kinds of events: *note events and non-note events*. A note event is the equivalent of pressing a piano key. It instructs the synthesizer to play a particular pitch at a precisely defined time. The command can convey musical nuances as well, such as how hard a piano key is struck, held down, or released. However, not all MIDI devices are designed to respond to this type of information.

Non-note events — sometimes called *controller events* or simply *controllers* — manage other functions of the MIDI device. They may, for example, adjust the volume or assign a new patch to one of the channels.

A MIDI file does not actually contain sound. Rather, it is a set of instructions that tell a synthesizer which sounds to make and when to make them. In this sense, a MIDI device is like a player piano and a MIDI sequence is like the perforated paper roll that controls it. If one of the holes instructs the piano to play the middle C key, the piano will do so.

The ultimate result, however, depends upon the quality and condition of the piano. If the middle C string is tuned to E-flat, you will hear E-flat. This sort of problem can occur with synthesizers, too, but the potential for error is even greater, since they can simulate so many different instruments.

Early Problems with MIDI

When it was first released, the MIDI specification attempted to strike a balance between standardization and versatility. MIDI manufacturers, software programmers, and composers agreed on certain basic commands, but other parts of the specification were less rigidly defined. With everyone free to play by their own rules, fundamental problems soon emerged:

File Format Though MIDI software programs could send and receive MIDI commands, each developed its own way of storing sequences on computer disks, so a MIDI file could be played only by the program that created it.

Patches The commands that tell the synthesizer which patches (instrument sounds) to use are really just numbers. Standardizing a numbering scheme was simple enough — patch numbers run from 0 to 127. But no rules governed which sound went with which number. Consequently, the part composed for violin on one synthesizer might sound like a trumpet when played on another.

Capabilities of the Synthesizer All hardware has inherent limits; a synthesizer can only make a certain number of sounds, and more importantly, it can only play a limited number of notes at once. These capabilities vary widely. A sequence created on a relatively powerful synthesizer — one that can simultaneously generate many notes and instruments — can overwhelm a lesser synthesizer.

These problems multiplied as the market grew. Patch and drum maps varied from one synthesizer manufacturer to another, or even among different models from the same manufacturer. The initial goal of MIDI — device-independent MIDI files that would play on any MIDI synthesizer — began to fade from view.

Working Toward Compatibility

To help composers create device-independent MIDI files, a number of organizations are at work to establish more fully-defined conventions. The MIDI Manufacturing Association has offered a specification called General MIDI (GM) which standardizes, among other things, instrument and drum sounds. The Multimedia PC Marketing Council, or MPC, divides synthesizers into two types — *Base Level* and *Extended Level* — so composers can tailor their arrangements to the differing capabilities of synthesizers.

Even if composers and manufacturers were to adopt a new standard today, incompatibility problems would remain for most of the MIDI devices and files already in use. As an interim solution, Microsoft created the MIDI Mapper — a software utility for Windows 3.1 that translates MIDI data as it is played, allowing newer files to work with older synthesizers.

With the release of Windows 95, Microsoft has replaced the MIDI Mapper with the MIDI Configuration utility. For more information on the MIDI Mapper and the Windows 95 Configuration utility, refer to their respective sections later in this chapter.

MIDI Terminology

What happens when a key on a MIDI keyboard is pressed? How is a MIDI command translated into the correct sound and routed to the correct destination? How is the sound created? The following section is designed to help you understand the fundamentals of synthesized sounds and how they are built into an entire composition.

We hope that these definitions are helpful to you as you begin to work with MIDI software.

Voices and Polyphony

Let's start with the most basic resource in a synthesizer, a *voice*. A voice is the electronic circuitry that can make a relatively simple sound. A synth that has more than one voice is said to be polyphonic. A synthesizer's *polyphony* — the number of voices — is a fundamental characteristic that establishes its capabilities. Virtually all synths made today are polyphonic.

Instruments and Timbre

A synth combines one or more voices to create an instrument — a sound that you hear and recognize, such as a piano, violin, tuba, or possibly a unique, newly invented sound. *Timbre* is the subjective, audible quality that distinguishes one instrument from another. Most synths are multi-timbral, that is, they can produce several different instrument sounds at once. This way you can have an entire band playing your composition.

Voices can usually be allocated dynamically. This means that when a voice is no longer needed, it immediately becomes available for another instrument. Occasionally, a MIDI arrangement calls for more voices than the synth can provide. Voices are then "stolen" from older notes to make the newer ones. For this reason, it's always a good idea to assign the more critical parts of an arrangement to lower-numbered MIDI channels. Voices are stolen from the higher numbered channels first.

Wavetable Synthesizers

Recently the technology of *wavetable synthesizers* has come into common use. These synthesizers use memory to store brief sound samples made from recordings of actual instruments. To play a note, the synthesizer looks up and retrieves the appropriate sample, manipulates it as needed and plays the sound. This system is considered to create more realistic instrument sounds, as opposed to the older FM (Frequency Modulation) synthesis technique of creating synthesized sound.

Patches

Each instrument sound is commonly called a *patch* or *program*. The terms are taken from the patch boards used to program early synthesizers. The operator used wires, like those on an old telephone switchboard, to "patch" or connect one electronic module to another. The words "patch," "instrument," "program" or sometimes simply "sound " are often used interchangeably.

Patches are usually identified by both a number and a recognizable name like "Marimba" or "Harpsichord." The numbers are always 0 to 127, though some systems label patches with numbers from 1 to 128 for clarity. A set of 128 patches is called a *patch bank* — or sometimes a *palette* — and many synths allow you to change patch banks as needed.

Notes

In MIDI, as in traditional music, a note is one of the most fundamental units. It defines a *pitch* (for example, F#) and a *duration* (for example, a half note). In MIDI, pitches are identified by numbers from 0 to 127. On many keyboards, for example, Middle C is note number 72. The duration is expressed in units of bars, beats and clicks. A click is the smallest division of a note according to the current MIDI configuration in a sequencer. As in traditional music, the duration of a note is ultimately determined by the key signature and the tempo of the song.

MIDI note commands define other characteristics, too. These include *start time* (which establishes where in the composition the note occurs) and *velocity* (which corresponds to how hard a key is struck).

Non-note Messages

Not all MIDI commands play notes; some control the overall characteristics of the song or the behavior of the synthesizer. These *non-note events* include commands that set the key signature and tempo, change patches, and a host of other parameters.

Each synthesizer will vary in its response to these messages, depending on its design and features. If a synth fails to respond to certain message types, it isn't necessarily a malfunction. It may simply be that the synth wasn't designed to support that feature.

Channels

Each MIDI note must be assigned to one of 16 channels. The note will then be played with the patch assigned to that channel. For example, if a violin patch has been assigned channel 4, all notes played on that channel will sound like violins. If you change the patch assignment for channel 4 to oboe, the sound changes to oboe.

Tracks

Imagine an arrangement that includes three clarinets playing in harmony. Since they all share the clarinet patch, they can share a channel. To assign the same patch to three different channels would waste the synth's resources. As you edit the arrangement, you need some way to keep the parts separate. In traditional music notation, you might put each part on its own staff.

The MIDI equivalent is to place each part on its own track. Each track must be assigned to a channel, and therefore a patch. The composer has considerable freedom in the use of tracks. Several tracks can be assigned to the same channel, and each track's channel assignment can be changed independently.

For example, suppose you decided to change one of the clarinet parts to an oboe, without changing the other two. You could assign its track to another channel — and assign an oboe patch to that channel.

Melodic and Percussion Instruments

There are two broad categories of instruments: *melodic instruments* and *percussion (drum) instruments*. Each melodic instrument requires a full range of notes, such as all the keys on the MIDI keyboard, and must have its own channel and patch assignment.

Percussion instruments, however, don't rely on pitch. You cannot play F-sharp on a cymbal or a snare drum the way you can on a piano or clarinet. So, while you need the entire range of the MIDI keyboard to play a melodic instrument like a piano, you only need a single key to play a cymbal.

Drum Channel

Because each drum instrument requires only one key, all the drums are gathered onto a single channel, and one key is assigned to trigger each. Every synthesizer has a *drum channel* for this purpose. This channel usually cannot be changed and is almost always channel 10 or 16.

If data created for a melodic instrument is inadvertently directed to the drum channel — or vice-versa — the synth attempts to play it anyway. The result is typically a strange collection of noises.

Ports

If there are only 16 channels — and each instrument claims one of them — how would you manage an arrangement that requires more than 16 instruments? This question leads us to the final parameter that MIDI data needs to reach its destination — a MIDI *port*.

Each set of 16 channels is assigned to a port, and a MIDI system can have several ports. Unlike channels and tracks, which are characteristics associated with MIDI data, ports are more closely associated with MIDI hardware. Ordinarily, each port is connected to a different MIDI device.

MIDI Hardware

To provide the ports necessary to control external MIDI devices, a computer requires hardware called a MIDI *interface*. An interface is typically a card installed in one of the bus slots on the computer's motherboard. It has one or more 5-pin DIN plugs to communicate with external MIDI devices. A cable connects the interface to a plug on the MIDI device. Each of these connections represents one MIDI port.

Each port is identified by a number and functions as an input or an output. Two-way communication requires both types. The computer receives data from a synthesizer (during recording) via an input port, and sends data to the synthesizer (during playback), via an output port. MIDI data travels only in one direction, so the MIDI Out plug from one device is always connected to the MIDI In of another. Multiport interfaces permit a single computer to control several 16-channel MIDI devices.

Many synths also have a specialized variant of the MIDI Out port, called *MIDI Thru*. A MIDI Thru simply takes the data that arrives at the MIDI In connector, echoes (repeats) it, and sends it out again, unchanged, via the MIDI Thru connector. This provides a useful way to connect several synthesizers together.

Sound Cards

Sound cards don't require a MIDI interface or a cable; the connection to the computer is established when the card is plugged into its slot. Since you cannot "play" a sound card as you would a keyboard, sound cards don't have a MIDI output port. Instead, they have connectors that send audio signals to devices such as headphones, speakers, or an amplifier.

However, many sound card designs allow for a simple kind of MIDI interface, so your computer can communicate with external MIDI devices in addition to the sound card. Usually it's an optional adapter cable that you plug into the sound card's joystick connector.

Every synth, whether it's internal (built into a sound card) or external (connected by means of an interface) must be identified by a port number. Since a sound card doesn't need an actual physical port, it's given a kind of artificial — or virtual — port assignment. The most common arrangement is to call the sound card's external MIDI connector Port 1 and the synthesizer built into the sound card Port 2. If your system had two external (real) ports, the virtual port for the sound card would be port 3, and so on.

Windows 3.1 MIDI Mapper

When you install MIDI hardware such as a sound card or a MIDI interface, an applet called the MIDI Mapper is added to your Windows 3.1 Control Panel.

Ordinarily, when you use a sequencer to play a MIDI file, you direct the output — the MIDI data — to the driver for your synthesizer. The driver manages the communication between the software application (the sequencer) and the hardware (the synthesizer).

The MIDI Mapper offers another option: instead of directing MIDI data to your synthesizer's driver, you can send it to the MIDI Mapper. To the Windows application, the MIDI Mapper appears to be a software driver.

The MIDI Mapper intercepts data from the software application and passes it on to your synthesizer's driver. What is the purpose of this extra step?

Before sending data along to the synth's driver, the MIDI Mapper can translate or re-map it. Depending on how you configure the MIDI Mapper, it can re-direct data (change its destination), it can halt data (prevent it from reaching your synthesizer) or it can just pass the data along unchanged. You can re-map channels, patch assignments and even individual keys — all independently of each other. This re-mapping function lets you reconcile differences between a MIDI file and your MIDI hardware.

For example, suppose all your MIDI files have drums on channel 10, but the drum channel on your synth is channel 16. You could use your sequencing software to open, edit and save every one of your files individually — changing channel 10 to channel 16, dozens or possibly hundreds of times.

A far less tedious solution would be to create a MIDI Mapper Setup that always re-maps data from channel 10 to channel 16. This approach offers two advantages:

- In one step you've made it possible for all the MIDI files to play on your synthesizer.
- Because you didn't alter the MIDI files, they will still play correctly on other synths.

The same file, in fact, can play correctly on any synth that has its own correctly configured setup. Because you can create and save as many setups as you wish and switch among them as needed, you can play the same file on a variety of synthesizers.

The Windows User's Guide and the MIDI Mapper's help file explain how to operate the MIDI Mapper. Consult these sources to set your MIDI Mapper correctly for your configuration.

 All your setups are saved in a single file called MIDIMAP.CFG in your WINDOWS\SYSTEM directory.

Always make a backup copy of MIDIMAP.CFG before you change any MIDI hardware or software.

Windows 95 MIDI Configuration Screen

Beginning with Windows 95, the MIDI Configuration dialog box replaces the MIDI Mapper utility, but it has different capabilities.

You can open the MIDI Configuration screen by selecting Multimedia from the Control Panel, then selecting the MIDI tab. In the MIDI Tab window you select the Custom Configuration option button and then click the Configure button. The MIDI Configuration dialog box opens.

Selecting a channel and clicking the Change button opens the Change MIDI Instrument Dialog box where you can set the driver assignments for the selected channel.

Appendix B

General MIDI

General MIDI Patch Set

The General MIDI Patch Set was designed to ensure compatibility between files by defining a common set of instrument names and MIDI numbers. This means, for example, that if you set a track to Patch #4, "Honky-tonk Piano," it should sound pretty much the same when played on any other General MIDI synthesizer or sound card.

These instrument sounds correspond to the numbers in the Patch column of MIDI Orchestrator Plus' Track/View screen.

For more information on setting patches, refer to the "Track/View Window," "Event Editor" and "Options Menu" chapters.

PIANO
1   Acoustic Grand Piano
2   Bright Acoustic Piano
3   Electric Grand Piano
4   Honky-tonk Piano
5   Rhodes Piano
6   Chorused Piano
7   Harpsichord
8   Clavinet Chromatic

PERCUSSION
9   Celesta
10 Glockenspiel
11 Music box
12 Vibraphone
13 Marimba
14 Xylophone
15 Tubular Bells
16 Dulcimer

ORGAN
17 Hammond Organ
18 Percussive Organ
19 Rock Organ
20 Church Organ
21 Reed Organ
22 Accordion
23 Harmonica
24 Tango Accordion

GUITAR
25 Acoustic Guitar (nylon)
26 Acoustic Guitar (steel)
27 Electric Guitar (jazz)
28 Electric Guitar (clean)
29 Electric Guitar (muted)
30 Overdriven Guitar
31 Distortion Guitar
32 Guitar Harmonics

BASS
33 Acoustic Bass
34 Electric Bass (finger)
35 Electric Bass (pick)
36 Fretless Bass
37 Slap Bass 1
38 Slap Bass 2
39 Synth Bass 1
40 Synth Bass 2

STRINGS
41 Violin
42 Viola
43 Cello
44 Contrabass
45 Tremolo Strings
46 Pizzicato Strings
47 Orchestral Harp
48 Timpani

ENSEMBLE
49 String Ensemble 1
50 String Ensemble 2
51 SynthStrings 1
52 SynthStrings 2
53 Choir Aahs
54 Voice Oohs
55 Synth voice
56 Orchestra Hit

BRASS
57 Trumpet
58 Trombone
59 Tuba
60 Muted Trumpet
61 French Horn
62 Brass Section
63 Synth Brass 1
64 Synth Brass 2

REED
65 Soprano Sax
66 Alto Sax
67 Tenor Sax
68 Baritone Sax
69 Oboe
70 English Horn
71 Bassoon
72 Clarinet

PIPE
73 Piccolo
74 Flute
75 Recorder
76 Pan Flute
77 Bottle Blow
78 Shakuhachi
79 Whistle
80 Ocarina

SYNTH LEAD
81 Lead 1 (square)
82 Lead 2 (sawtooth)
83 Lead 3 (calliope lead)
84 Lead 4 (chiff lead)
85 Lead 5 (charang)
86 Lead 6 (voice)
87 Lead 7 (fifths)
88 Lead 8 (bass + lead)

SYNTH PAD
89 Pad 1 (new age)
90 Pad 2 (warm)
91 Pad 3 (polysynth)
92 Pad 4 (choir)
93 Pad 5 (bowed)
94 Pad 6 (metallic)
95 Pad 7 (halo)
96 Pad 8 (sweep)

SYNTH EFFECTS
97 FX 1 (rain)
98 FX 2 (soundtrack)
99 FX 3 (crystal)
100 FX 4 (atmosphere)
101 FX 5 (brightness)
102 FX 6 (goblins)
103 FX 7 (echoes)
104 FX 8 (sci-fi)

ETHNIC
105 Sitar
106 Banjo
107 Shamisen
108 Koto
109 Kalimba
110 Bagpipe
111 Fiddle
112 Shanai

PERCUSSIVE
113 Tinkle Bell
114 Agogo
115 Steel Drums
116 Woodblock
117 Taiko Drum
118 Melodic Tom
119 Synth Drum
120 Reverse Cymbal

SOUND EFFECTS
121 Guitar Fret Noise
122 Breath Noise
123 Seashore
124 Bird Tweet
125 Telephone
126 Helicopter
127 Applause
128 Gunshot

General MIDI Drum Note Map

Like the General MIDI Patch Set, the General MIDI Drum Note Map ensures that the drums you designate in your MIDI file will sound the same when played back on other General MIDI sound cards or synthesizers.

The drum sounds correspond to the piano keys on the vertical keyboard in the Piano Roll screen. If you have a General MIDI (GM) instrument and set the track to Channel 10, these drum sounds will play when you insert notes in the Piano Roll screen.

In the table below, the left column indicates the MIDI numbers, the middle column represents the keys in the Piano Roll window or on a MIDI instrument, and the right column displays the corresponding drum sounds.

35	B2	Acoustic Bass Drum
36	C3	Bass Drum 1
37	C#3	Side Stick
38	D3	Acoustic Snare
39	D#3	Hand Clap
40	E3	Electric Snare
41	F3	Low Floor Tom
42	F#3	Closed Hi-Hat
43	G3	Hi Floor Tom
44	G#3	Pedal Hi-Hat
45	A3	Low Tom
46	A#3	Open Hi Hat
47	B3	Low-Mid Tom
48	C4	High-Mid Tom
49	C#4	Crash Cymbal 1
50	D4	High Tom
51	D#4	Ride Cymbal 1
52	E4	Chinese Cymbal
53	F4	Ride Bell
54	F#4	Tambourine
55	G4	Splash Cymbal
56	G#4	Cowbell
57	A4	Crash Cymbal 2
58	A#4	Vibraslap

59	B4	Ride Cymbal 2
60	C5	High Bongo
61	C#5	Low Bongo
62	D5	Mute High Conga
63	D#5	Open High Conga
64	E5	Low Conga
65	F5	High Timbale
66	F#5	Low Timbale
67	G5	High Agogo
68	G#5	Low Agogo
69	A5	Cabasa
70	A#5	Maracas
71	B5	Short Whistle
72	C6	Long Whistle
73	C#6	Short Guiro
74	D6	Long Guiro
75	D#6	Claves
76	E6	High Wood Block
77	F6	Low Wood Block
78	F#6	Mute Cuica
79	G6	Open Cuica
80	G#6	Mute Triangle
81	A6	Open Triangle

General MIDI Controller Types

General MIDI Controller Types are specified with numbers from 0-127 and control various instrument parameters such as pitch bend, effects depth, and volume. For additional information on using these controller types, refer to the "Parameters for Controller Events" section in the "Event Editor" chapter and "Controller A and Controller B Settings" in the "Track/View Window" and "Mixer Window" chapters.

#	NAME	POSSIBLE VALUES
1	MOD WHEEL	0 - 127
2	BREATH	0 - 127
4	FOOT PEDAL	0 - 127
5	PORTAMENTO TIME	0 - 127
6	DATA SLIDER	0 - 127
7	MAIN VOLUME	0 - 127
8	CONTINUOUS RELEASE	0 - 127
10	PAN	0 - 127
11	EXPRESSION CONTROL	0 - 127
64	SUSTAIN	0 = off/127 = on
65	PORTAMENTO SWITCH	0 = off /127 = on
66	SUSTENUTO SWITCH	0 = off /127 = on
67	SOFT SWITCH	0 = off /127 = on
68	2ND RELEASE SWITCH	0 = off /127 = on
84	PORTAMENTO	0 - 127
91	EFFECTS 1 DEPTH	0 - 127 (Normally Reverb)
92	EFFECTS 2 DEPTH	0 - 127
93	EFFECTS 3 DEPTH	0 - 127 (Normally Chorus)
94	EFFECTS 4 DEPTH	0 - 127
95	EFFECTS 3 DEPTH	0 - 127
96	DATA PLUS	0 = off/127 = on
97	DATA MINUS	0 = off/127 = on
121	RESET ALL CONTROLLERS	normally 0
123	ALL NOTES OFF	normally 0
124	OMNI MODE OFF	normally 0
125	OMNI MODE ON	normally 0
126	MONO MODE ON	0/all voices to mono
127	POLY MODE ON	normally 0

Appendix C

Shortcut Keys

These shortcut keys make MIDI Orchestrator Plus easier to use.

Transport Bar Shortcut Keys

The Transport Buttons (Rewind, Stop, Play, Record, Pause, and Fast Forward) have been duplicated on the keys F4- F9, in the same order from left to right

KEY	TRANSPORT BUTTON FUNCTIONS
F4	Rewind
F5	Stop
F6	Play
F7	Record
F8	Pause
F9	Fast Forward
Shift + F4	Rapid rewind
Shift + F9	Rapid fast forward
Shift + F7	Toggles punch key
Shift + F6	Plays current range

Other Shortcut Keys

These keys help you move throughout the program.

KEY	FUNCTION
F1	Help
F2	Patch or Port selection
F3	Toggle field or column width (Name, Port, Patch, Volume)
Ctrl + Tab	Jumps to any MIDI Orchestrator Plus window
Tab	Toggles between the Track pane and the Bar pane
Ctrl + X	Cut
Ctrl + C	Copy
Ctrl + V	Paste
Ctrl + D	Delete
Ctrl + A	Select All
Ctrl + Z	Undo
Ctrl + R	Redo
Ctrl + N	Go to Next Track in Piano Roll and Event Editor
Ctrl + P	Go to Previous Track in Piano Roll and Event Editor
Ctrl + T	Set focus to Tempo
Ctrl + O	Open File
Ctrl + S	Save File
Alt + F4	Exit the Program
Spacebar	Starts/Stops Playing Selection

Appendix D

Changing Numericals

To change the values in boxes with spin buttons, you can use the spin buttons alone or in conjunction with the Shift and Ctrl keys.

To Increase a Value...

Action	Where	Effect
Click the mouse button	on an up Spin Button	to increase the value by the smallest amount.
Press the + key	when a numerical box is selected	to increase the value by the smallest amount.
Hold the Ctrl key and press the + key	when a numerical box is selected	to increase the value to the maximum amount.
Hold the Shift key and click the mouse button	on an up Spin button	to increase the value by a large amount.

| Press the multiply * key | when a numerical box is selected | to increase the value by a large amount. |
| Hold the Ctrl key and click the mouse button | on an up Spin button | to increase the value to the maximum amount. |

To Decrease a Value...

Action	*Where*	*Effect*
Click the mouse button	on a down Spin Button	to decrease the value by the smallest amount.
Press the – key	when a numerical box is selected	to decrease the value by the smallest amount.
Hold the Ctrl key and press the – key	when a numerical box is selected	to decrease the value to the minimum amount.
Hold the Shift key and click the mouse button	on a down Spin button	to decrease the value by a large amount.
Press the divide / key	when a numerical box is selected	to decrease the value by a large amount.
Hold the Ctrl key and click the mouse button	on a down Spin button	to decrease the value to the minimum amount.

Appendix E

Troubleshooting

Fortunately, the situations that cause the most multimedia problems are among the easiest to fix. Start your troubleshooting journey with the general suggestions below. If you still have problems, look up the specific symptoms you're experiencing.

Throughout the troubleshooting process, don't forget another valuable resource — the hardware manuals that came with your sound card or other peripherals.

First, confirm that your sound card is connected to a working output device such as headphones, speakers or an amplifier with speakers. If you are using speakers, make certain that they:

- Are plugged into the correct port on your sound card.
- Are turned on and have the volume set to an adequate level.
- Have their own source of power. Most sound cards can supply enough power for headphones, but not for external speakers. Depending on the type, your speakers will need to be plugged into a wall outlet or an amplifier, or will be powered by batteries.

If the speakers are not the problem, then you will have to check your multimedia devices. To do so, you can use:

- Windows® Media Player
- Voyetra's MediaCheck™

Media Player

There are three devices you can test using the Windows Media Player: the MIDI Sequencer, digital audio (Sound), and Video.

To open the Media Player in Windows 3.1:

1. Double-click the Accessories program group.
2. Double-click the Media Player icon.

To open the Media Player in Windows 95:

1. Click Start.
2. Point to Programs. Point to Accessories. Point to Multimedia.
3. Click Media Player. Media Player opens.

To test multimedia devices with Media Player:

1. Click Device to display the multimedia devices on your system. If you do not see Sound, Video for Windows or MIDI Sequencer listed in the menu, they are not properly installed on your system. Refer to your user's manual or contact your hardware manufacturer for assistance.
2. Click the name of the device — Sound, Video for Windows, or MIDI Sequencer — you want to test.
3. Locate a file of the type of media you want to test and click Open.
4. Click the Play button. If you hear the sound or MIDI or see the video, the drivers are installed and working properly. If any of these multimedia devices fail to operate correctly, contact your hardware manufacturer.

Setting the Mixer

Some of the basic problems that occur with multimedia applications can easily be remedied by checking the Windows 95 mixer. With the mixer, you can control the volume of the different components on your computer's sound system.

Windows 3.1 does not include a mixer, although many sound cards include mixer applications for Windows 3.1. If you are running Windows 3.1, check your sound card's documentation to determine if you have a mixer and how to access it.

To open the mixer in Windows 95:

1. Click Start.
2. Point to Programs. Point to Accessories. Point to Multimedia.
3. Click Volume Control. Make any necessary changes from the Volume Control Panel.

Possible Mixer Problems

" The sound is too low or I don't hear any sounds at all. "

" Some of my components work, but others do not. For example, I can hear MIDI but I cannot hear WAV (digital audio)."

Possible Problem

The mixer settings are too low or some of the components are muted.

Possible Solution

Check the mixer to make sure all of the components' volumes are at least half way to the top. Also, check that none of the components are muted. In particular, check the Master volume setting if there is one.

❝ MIDI and WAV (digital audio) files do not play simultaneously. ❞

Possible Problem

The sound card cannot support the simultaneous playing of MIDI and WAV.

Possible Solution

Open two instances of Media Player. In one play a MIDI file, in the other play a WAV file. If they do not play simultaneously, contact your sound card manufacturer.

Troubleshooting MIDI

❝ I can't find the connectors to hook my sound card and my MIDI keyboard together. ❞

Possible Problem

Your keyboard is not a MIDI device. Not all synthesizers or electronic keyboards support MIDI.

Possible Solution

Look for round MIDI plugs labeled MIDI IN, MIDI OUT or MIDI THRU. They are usually found on the back panel of the MIDI keyboard. If your keyboard is not equipped with these plugs, you will not be able to hook your keyboard to your computer.

Possible Problem

Your sound card did not come with a MIDI connector cable.

Possible Solution

Most sound cards don't have MIDI connectors. A special adapter cable that connects to the joystick port is used instead. The manufacturer of your sound card can probably provide you with one, or you can purchase one from Voyetra.

" I'm getting sound, but it there's interference with it. "

Possible Problem

A hum, hissing or other constant undertone of noise usually indicates electrical interference or a hardware malfunction.

Possible Solution

Increase the sound card's output level and lower the amplifier's volume. If that doesn't help, try it the other way around.

If you are not able to resolve this problem, contact the hardware manufacturer.

" Music files that work with other Windows programs or tracks from my CD player won't load into MIDI Orchestrator Plus. "

Possible Problem

You tried to open a file that isn't supported by MIDI Orchestrator Plus.

Possible Solution

Be sure the file is a valid MIDI file with a .MID, or .ORC extension. Digitally recorded sound files — those with .WAV, .VOC extensions, or CD Audio Tracks — can't be used by a MIDI sequencer.

" I cannot record from my MIDI keyboard. "

" I do not hear anything when I play my MIDI keyboard. "

Possible Problem

Your sound card isn't connected to an output.

Possible Solution

Be sure your sound card is connected to a working output device such as headphones, speakers or an amplifier with speakers — and that you are using self-powered speakers. The sound card's amp isn't designed to power external speakers.

Possible Problem

Your MIDI cables are not plugged in correctly.

Possible Solution

Make sure that the MIDI cable runs from the MIDI keyboard's MIDI Out to the computer's MIDI In and vice versa.

Possible Problem

Your synthesizer is not set up to transmit MIDI.

Possible Solution

Some MIDI instruments send and/or receive MIDI data automatically, or can be configured to do so. Others require that you take specific steps to transmit MIDI each time you turn on the synthesizer. Check your MIDI instrument's instructions to find out how to set it up to transmit MIDI. The salesperson who sold you the MIDI instrument may also be helpful.

Possible Problem

Your synthesizer and computer are set to different MIDI ports and/or channels.

Possible Solution

Make sure that MIDI Orchestrator Plus is set to receive on the same channel that your synthesizer is using to send MIDI data. Most synthesizers use channel 1 by default.

Make sure the Port in MIDI Orchestrator Plus's Port column matches the Port your MIDI instrument is connected to—or the name of the sound driver you want to use.

In the Track/View Screen, find the track or tracks you want to play back and click on the Port box to change it to the right port for your instrument (or the driver you're using).

If you now need to choose a different driver, open the Options Menu to see what MIDI drivers you have available. Now select your MIDI Port choice.

Possible Problem

The MIDI drivers are not properly configured.

Possible Solution

Run MediaCheck to diagnose and fix the problem.

Possible Problem

There is no power to the MIDI keyboard.

Possible Solution

Check to make sure the MIDI keyboard is plugged in and turned on.

" I can hear music when I play my MIDI keyboard, but I can't record. "

Possible Problem

You have not selected a track for recording.

Possible Solution

Be sure that at least one track shows the letter "R" in the Record column.

Possible Problem

Your synthesizer is sending on one channel and/or port and the software is set to receive on another.

Possible Solution

Be sure you know which port and channel your synth is using to send MIDI data, and set the track you've selected for recording has the same settings.

“ When playing a MIDI file I don't hear anything. ”

Possible Problem

The MIDI file is an Extended Level file and your sound card is set up for Base Level, or vice-versa.

Possible Solution

Run MediaCheck to help diagnose and resolve the problem.

Possible Problem

The wrong output port is selected in the MIDI Port Setup dialog box.

Possible Solution

Check that the correct MIDI Port is selected in the Port Column of the Track/View screen.

“ When I change the patch on one track, some of the other tracks change too. ”

Possible problem

You have assigned several tracks to the same channel. (This isn't really a problem—the program is designed to work this way.)

Possible solution

Assign the track to a different channel. Patches are assigned to *channels*, not to tracks, so when you change a patch, you change it for every track assigned to that channel.

“ When I play the MIDI keyboard, I hear a strange echo or the notes sound doubled-up — thicker. Sometimes I run out of voices and not all the notes sound. ”

Possible problem

Your MIDI file contains a Base-Level and an Extended Level arrangement, and you're trying to play both of them at the same time.

Possible solution

Set the MIDI Mapper in Windows 3.1, or the MIDI Configuration in Windows 95, to play only channels 1 through 10, or only channels 13 through 16. MediaCheck can help you determine which option is correct for your situation.

Possible problem

The MIDI data arriving at the MIDI In is echoed to the MIDI Out.

Possible solution

In the Options menu, try turning MIDI Thru off. If it stops, you've found the problem. If you are using a keyboard controller, try turning the local control off. See the documentation for the keyboard to do this.

" It sounds as if tracks are missing from my MIDI file. Also, other parts sound very strange and there are no drum sounds. "

Possible Problem

Your MIDI Mapper in Windows 3.1 or the MIDI Configuration in Windows 95 is not set up properly; you're trying to play an Extended-Level arrangement on a Base-Level synth.

Possible Solution

In Windows 3.1, check that the MIDI Mapper is set up correctly for your sound card.

In Windows 95, check that the MIDI configuration is set up correctly for your sound card.

Possible Problem

The file could just be too complex for your synth.

Possible Solution

Edit the file so it doesn't demand as many simultaneous notes and/or instruments from your synth.

❝ When trying to display or print notation, I don't see characters that look like music. ❞

Possible Problem

The font required for notation is not correctly installed.

Possible Solution

Make sure the Voyetra True Type notation font—SPW.TTF is installed correctly. Use the Windows Control Panel to install the font.

If SPW True Type is listed in the FONTS applet in Control Panel, but the file shows 0k bytes or you encounter some other problem, the file may have been corrupted. Highlight the file, click the remove button and then re-install the font by clicking on the Add button. Highlight SPW True Type and click OK. The SPW.TTF file can be found in the root directory of the CD.

Also, make sure you have the latest drivers installed for your printer. Contact your printer manufacturer for more information about your printer drivers.

❝ I try to display notation, but when I click the Transcribe button and click on OK, nothing happens and nothing is displayed. ❞

Possible Problem

You have not selected a track, or the tracks you've selected don't contain any notes.

Possible Solution

In the Transcription window, select one or more tracks that contain MIDI note data.

Troubleshooting Video

❝ Videos do not play. ❞

Possible Problem
Video for Windows is not installed.

Possible Solution
Run SETUPFW.EXE from the VFW directory on the CD.

❝ I can see the video, but I do not hear any sound. ❞

Possible Problem
Your mixer is set too low.

Possible Solution
Check the mixer and increase the output volume setting for WAV.

❝ My video playback skips. ❞

❝ The sound and the video are not in sync. ❞

Possible Problem
Your system is too slow.

Possible Solution
Close any other applications which are open. Also, close any TSRs (Terminate and Stay Resident programs) such as screen savers.

Use a 2x (double-speed) or faster CD-ROM.

Troubleshooting WAV (Digital Audio)

" I cannot hear any digital audio. "

Possible Problem

You do not have the correct drivers installed.

Possible Solution

Check to make sure you have the latest drivers for your sound card. This can be done with MediaCheck.

Run Media Player and test the device labeled Sound. If Sound does not work, contact your sound card manufacturer.

" The sound sometimes stutters and/or stops. "

Possible Problem

Your system may be too slow. The demands of recording and editing digital audio can tax many computer components, particularly older, slower ones.

Possible Solution

Close any open applications.

Check to make sure you have the latest drivers for your sound card.

" The sound is garbled. "

Possible Problem

If sound suddenly stops or "stutters," and/or locks up your computer, you probably have a hardware conflict—more than one device trying to use the same IRQ, I/O address or DMA channel.

Possible Solution

Check your user's manual or contact your hardware manufacturer for help on how to resolve these type of problems.

Appendix F

Technical Support

If you have reviewed the "Troubleshooting" section of this manual, used MediaCheck, and can play a MIDI file and a WAV file with the Windows Media Player, but cannot do so when you are using any of the applications in MIDI Orchestrator Plus, here's how to contact Technical Support.

- **Voyetra on the Internet**
  E-mail us at support@voyetra.com

- **Voyetra Forum on CompuServe®**
  Type GO VOYETRA at any prompt
  or leave an e-mail message for user ID: 76702.2037

- **Voyetra's Bulletin Board**
  Contact us at 914-966-1216 (any modem speed up to 28,800 baud, 8 bits, 1 stop bit, no parity, ANSI emulation). Post your message or question and we'll answer within a few days. Our Bulletin Board contains useful tips from other users, news about upcoming products and more.

- **Telephone Technical Support**
  For urgent problems, contact Voyetra's Technical Support at 914-966-0600.

Before You Call

- If possible, use a phone near your computer and have the application running.
- We might need to ask about the hardware installed in your system — the sound card, synthesizer, MIDI interface or other devices you are using. Try to have the manufacturer's manuals nearby.

Be prepared to explain what you were doing when the problem occurred and any error messages you received.

 You will need the Product ID number if you phone for Technical Support. You should have written this number on the first page of this manual.

However, if you didn't, this number can be found on the top half of the Registration Card which came with the software or in the About box for MIDI Orchestrator Plus.

Index

F

G

H

I

N

Q

Quantize · 83
  Note Duration · 166
  Note Start Time · 166
Quick View Buttons · 15, 23, 26, 53

R

R Column · 50
Range · 30
  Looping · 49
  Recording · 50
  Selecting · 30
Readme file · 8
Receive Button · 144
Record · 15, 45
Record Button · 34, 35
Record Enable · 61
Record Punch In Button · 50, 51
Record Status · 53
Recording
  From Middle of a Song · 51
  MIDI · 34, 61
  Multitrack · 36, 61
  New Track · 34
  Range · 50
  Saving with a new name · 37
  Stopping · 35
Redo · 157, 163, 216
Refresh · 75, 191
Registering your software · ii
  benefits of · 2
Reset Controllers · 176
Rest Suppression · 84
Restore Window Button · 25
Rests · 82
Reverb · 65
Reverse · 163
Rewind · 15, 45, 215

RIFF File · *See* File format
Ritardando · 56, 133
RMI Files · *See* File Format
Rounded Notes · 97
Ruler Area · 87

S

Sample files · 4, 39
SAMPLE.ORC · 4, 27, 29, 35
  saving · 52
Save · 142
Save As command · 150
Save Button · 141
Save command · 150
Save Settings on Exit · 38, 96, 170
Saving Your Recording · 37
Select All command · 159
Send Button · 143
Send Reset Controllers on Stop ·
  176
Separator Symbols · 47, 48
Sequence · 197
Sequencer · 197
Set Velocity · 165
Shortcut keys · 215
Show Column · 79
Shrink All · 59
Shrink Columns · 32
silences · 82, 105
Snap Grid On/Off · 93
Snap-to-Grid · 92
SNG · 152
Software
  Closing · 38
  Configuring · 12
Solo · 32, 33, 64, 65, 104, 105, 106
Solo Button · 105
Solo Column · 33
Song
  building · 39

Workspace · 13, 16, 23
World Wide Web address · ii, 2

Z

Zoom · 76
Zoom Control · 95
Zoom Percentage Dialog Box · 76